ORGANIZATIONAL VALUES, VISION AND CULTURE

New Perspectives

ORGANIZATIONAL VALUES, VISION AND CULTURE

New Perspectives

Editors

Dr. M. ANBALAGAN
Reader and Head

Dr. A. ARULAPPAN
Reader in Commerce

Post Graduate and Research Department of Commerce
Voorhees College, Vellore

Foreword

Dr. P. JEGADISH GANDHI
Founder Director
Vellore Institute of Development Studies (VIDS)
Vellore
Professor of Economics, Voorhees College (1970-2000)

DEEP & DEEP PUBLICATIONS PVT. LTD.
F-159, Rajouri Garden, New Delhi - 110 027

ORGANIZATIONAL VALUES, VISION AND CULTURE
New Perspectives

ISBN 978-81-8450-188-9

Printed in India at MAYUR ENTERPRISES
WZ Plot No. 3, Gujjar Market, Tihar Village, New Delhi - 110 018

Published by DEEP & DEEP PUBLICATIONS PVT. LTD.,
F-159, Rajouri Garden, New Delhi - 110 027 • Phone : 25435369, 25440916
E-mail : ddpubs@gmail.com • ddpbooks@yahoo.co.in
Showroom :
2/13, Ansari Road, Daryaganj, New Delhi - 110 002 • Telefax : 23245122

Contents

Part II

ORGANIZATIONAL CULTURE DIALECTICS : A PERISCOPIC VIEW

Part III

ORGANIZATIONAL DYNAMICS : A MICRO VIEW

PART IV

ORGANIZATIONAL LIFE : A HOLISTIC VIEW

PART V

ORGANIZATIONAL DEVELOPMENT : A FOCAL VIEW

Foreword

The concept of "Organizational Culture" has gained new perspective changes in the post-globalised socio-economic system. Managers in both the public and private sectors are investing growing amounts of time and energy in planning and managing organizational changes in terms of its values and culture.

This edited volume contains the papers of experts and young academics presented at the 2-day UGC-sponsored National Seminar on "Organizational Values, Vision and Culture" conducted by PG and Research Department of Commerce, Voorhees College, Vellore in April 2008.

Since its inception of the Department of Commerce in 1970s, I have been associated with its all programmes. I admired the growth and development of the Department from the UG level to PG level with research facilities under the stewardship of Professors late Dr. K.V. Viswanathan and Dr. P. Arunachalam with the guidance of Dr. M.J. John, former Principal. Really pleased to know that the same spirit and activities are being pursued under the dynamic leadership of Dr. M. Anbalagan with a dedicated team of staff members.

I congratulate the editors, Dr. M. Anbalagan and Dr. A. Arulappan for their sincere effort in bringing out a compiled work for the benefit of management experts, academics and students and research scholars.

Dr. P. JEGADISH GANDHI
Founder Director
Vellore Institute of Development Studies (VIDS)
Vellore
Professor of Economics, Voorhees College (1970-2000)

Preface

Every organization operates with certain values, long-term vision and culture expressed by its employees and others in their activities. There may or may not be a conscious effort on the part of their CEOs or employees to pursue them specifically all the time. But by an overview, one can perceive the existence of the Organizational Values, Vision and Culture (in each and every organization OVVC). Change of CEOs, employees and technology may influence a change in the pattern of OVVC. Some values become non-operational and priority of certain others changes the corporate vision remains focused or modified and the culture of operations gets changed to meet certain newly emerging needs.

The OVVC are relevant to large, medium, small business organizations and also to educational institutions which are service-oriented. Since many educational institutions are determined to create a surplus, they have also become profit-oriented organizations.

The book contains papers presented at the Seminar which was held at the Voorhees College, Vellore on 15-16 April, 2008. The selected papers found to be more relevant are published. It is our hope that the readers will appreciate the significance of the theme and try to adopt the same in their organization.

We record our thanks to the University Grant Commission for its grant, which has enabled us to organize the programme. We are grateful to the Management of Voorhees College under the Chairmanship of the Rt. Rev. Dr. Y. William, Bishop of CSI

Vellore and the Principal and Secretary of our College Dr. D. Daniel Ezhilarasu for their support and guidance in making this national event to take place in our college.

We wish to acknowledge our sincere gratitude to our erudite Professor Dr. D. Amarchand, former Registrar of University of Madras for his support, valuable guidance and encouragement in conducting the National Seminar and also, his expertise in bringing out this book. We are indebted to him for his teachings and guidings which enabled us to attempt this academic endeavor.

Dr. P. Jegadish Gandhi, Director, VIDS, a moving force, venturing on resolving many social issues and problems, has accepted to write a Foreword for this book. We gratefully acknowledge him with thanks and we are sure that his foreword would have electrifying effect on this academic exercise in future as well.

We are highly obliged to all the chairpersons of the theme sessions of the seminar, for their valuable contributions which, adorns important part of the book. We sincerely express our gratitude to all the participants. We wish to appreciate the delegates whose papers are included in this book.

We also record our thanks to Ms. V. Renuka, Lecturer in English, for her efforts in meticulously proof reading the entire manuscript and we also acknowledge the services of Mr. S. Murugan, Lecturer in Commerce, Voorhees College, Vellore for executing neatly word processing work.

Our special thanks are due to M/s. Deep & Deep Publications (P) Ltd., whose sincere efforts brought this book in such an excellent get up and being a channel in spreading the message of the theme across the academic circles and the organization builders.

Dr. M. ANBALAGAN
Dr. A. ARULAPPAN

List of Contributors

Dr. A. Arulappan, Reader in Commerce, Voorhees College, Vellore.

Ms. C.S. Vijaya, Lecturer, SDNB Vaishnav College for Women, Chrompet, Chennai.

Mr. C.V. Gopal, LIC of India, Chennai.

Dr. D. Amarchand, Prof. & Head, Department of Commerce and Registrar, University of Madras—Retd.

Mr. D. Paulraj, Lecturer (SG) in Commerce, Voorhees College, Vellore.

Mr. G. Viswanathan, Chancellor, Vellore Institute of Technology, Deemed University, Vellore.

Mrs. G. Tamil Selvi, Lecturer, SDNB Vaishnav College for Women, Chrompet, Chennai.

Dr. H.R. Venkatesha, Director, Achariya Institute of Sciences, Center for Management Studies, Bangalore.

Dr. J. Srinivasan, Lecturer (SS) in Commerce, Arignar Anna Government Arts College, Cheyyar.

Thiru. K.S. Krithivasan, Addl. General Manager, Bharat Heavy Electricals Ltd., Ranipet.

Mrs. L. Anusha, Lecturer in Commerce, Sri Rajeswari College of Arts & Science for Women, Bonımaiyapalayam, Vanur.

Dr. M. Akbar Mohideen, Reader in Corporate Secretaryship, C. Abdul Hakeem College, Melvisharam.

Dr. M. Anbalagan, Reader and Head, PG Dept. of Commerce, Voorhees College, Vellore.

Mr. M.A. Krishnamurthy, Lecturer, Dr. MGR Chokalingam Arts College, Arni.

Dr. Md. Galib Hussain, Professor and Head of the Department of Corporate Secretaryship, Islamiya College, Vaniyambadi.

Ms. M. Lakshmi Priya, Student, Voorhees College, Vellore.

Mrs. M. Rajeswari, Sr. Lecturer and Research Scholar, Dept. of Commerce, Guru Shree Shanthivijai Jain College for Women, Vepery, Chennai.

Ms. M. Venkata Chaitanya, Student, VIT Business School, VIT University, Vellore.

Ms. N. Shivapriya, Student, VIT Business School, VIT University, Vellore.

Mr. N. Md. Faiyas Ahmed, Lecturer in Commerce, Mazharul Uloom College, Ambur.

Mr. P. Anbalagan, Lecturer in Economics, Voorhees College, Vellore.

Ms. P.D. Rajeswari, Lecturer, Dept. of Corporate Secretaryship, Anna Adarsh College for Women, Chennai.

Mr. P.M. Aadil Ahmed, Lecturer (SG) and Research Scholar, Dept. of Corporate Secretaryship, Mazharul Uloom College, Ambur.

Mr. R. Rangarajan, Lecturer, Dept. of Commerce, Dr. MGR Janaki College, Chennai.

Ms. R. Padmaja, Lecturer (SS) in Commerce, DKM College for Women, Vellore.

Ms. R. Subashini, Lecturer, VIT Business School, VIT University, Vellore.

Ms. R. Usha, Head, Dept. of Commerce, Dr. MGR Janaki College, Chennai.

Mr. S. Abdul Sajid, Lecturer SG in Commerce, C. Abdul Hakeem College, Melvisharam.

Dr. S. Booma, Reader, Dept. of Commerce, JBAS College, Chennai.

Mr. S. Kamalakkannan, Guest Lecturer, Dept. of Commerce, Government Arts College, Tiruvannamalai.

Dr. S. Kayalvizhi, Asst. Professor, School of Management, C. Abdul Hakeem College of Engg. & Technology, Melvisharam.

Dr. S. Shamsuddin, Reader in Commerce, C. Abdul Hakeem College, Melvisharam.

Mr. T. Afsar Basha, Lecturer (SS) in Commerce, Islamiah College, Vaniyambadi.

Prof. V. Gugaraman, Director—MBA, Thirumalai Engineering College, Kanchipuram.

Ms. V. Shenbagapriya, Head, Dept. of Commerce, Marudhar Kesri Jain College for Women, Vaniyambadi.

PART I

Organizational Values, Vision and Culture—A Macro View

Nurturing Innovative Culture

G. Viswanathan

It is always a joyous occasion to come back to my alma mater and this is the hall, the auditorium, where first I started addressing as a student 53 years ago. I am happy that Dr. Anbalagan, has chosen this important topic, "Organizational Values, Vision and Culture" for this National Seminar. The other day, Saturday the 12th April, I was invited to deliver a talk at Madras, in a Conference organized by CII (Confederation of Indian Industry) and the topic was Vision 20-25 for Tamilnadu. I was dealing with how the education scenario will be in 20-25 of Tamilnadu focusing on the strategies for Government as well as the Educational Institutions. The same exercise was done by many experts on infrastructure, health care, agriculture, rural development, etc. Efforts put in by various experts to prepare vision document for Tamilnadu gives me confidence that we are in the right track. The destination is known and the path is also laid up. Success depends on the travel. Fast or slow, jumping or leaping in a harmonious way or in a chaotic way. We continue to journey or stop in between. Everything depends on us. I am indeed very happy that Voorhees College has thought about an optic and important topic like this, to orient all the educational institutions towards the right direction. In the 21st century world competition is a prime factor everywhere. Changing ourselves to catch up the best practices in an innovative way is the only way for success.

COMPETITION, CHANGE AND INNOVATION

I request all of you to kindly remember these three important words and retain it in your mind for success. They are 'Competition', 'Change' and 'Innovation'. Similar to the vision documents prepared for India in 20-20 and for Tamilnadu in 20-25, every educational institution or business organization should have a vision document. This should focus on how we want our institutions to be in the next 20-25 years? It is a well known fact that without vision, an individual or organization will perish. Vision usually is the motivating factor for all of us to move forward. Without vision, people sometime strangulate or even record negative growth; even if positive growth is there, it will be very slow or it will be a slow growth, which will not make one a winner.

NEED FOR INNOVATIVE CULTURE

Before coming to vision statement a thorough study on the world around and the direction and speed with which the world is moving should be studied and understood. The exact need has to be articulated and the strength of the organization is to be assessed. Even though the leader has the major say for formulation of vision, it is necessary that all the people in the system are involved in the process of formulation of vision to have a better acceptability. For example, even though the principal is the main factor in a college, the members of the faculty and the students are to be involved for making a vision statement. The vision statement formulated should reflect the values of the organization and institution. Values are something that one believes, that it is more important. Some of the organizational values are ethics, excellence, helping, harmony, money, sophistication, time, people, etc. What pride one has towards the vision is determined by the value system? If money is one's value system, he would have the vision to be one among the fortune 500 companies of the world in the next 20 or 25 years. If one's value is going to people, then the vision will be to become an institution of excellence in producing human capital. All the educational institutions will be in this category. If one's value system is helping, then his vision is something similar to making 10,000 marginalized children to get degree for the next 10 years and so on. At VIT University, we have clear vision to become one among the top 100 universities in the world for next 15-20 years and this vision is based on our values, namely the people, the value of our students and employees and teachers more than anything else. I am confident with our value system we will be able to reach the pinnacle very soon. How fast we reach our destination depends on the culture we nurture in the organization. It is said that 80% of the organizational culture is attributable to the leadership behaviour depends on the top person; chancellor, vice-chancellor, principal, etc. That is, the management and faculty members of the educational institutions are responsible for the culture prevailing in the institution. What kind of work culture are you going to provide? Because, we are preparing the youngsters for the future. So they must be prepared to work at any time for hard work. I find that the work culture in India comparatively in Tamilnadu is far better than many other states. We have our entrance examination on 19th April. Out of 1,38,000 applications received, around 80,000 applications came from the northern Hindi-speaking states. When I asked the parents why do you want to put your children here? They told that the work culture and discipline is far better in Tamilnadu than anywhere in India. That's why they wanted to put their children here. And we need to be the role models. The management and the teachers are to be the role models. Very often the children follow the teachers rather than the parents. At VIT University we are attempting to articulate, inculcate innovative culture among every one.

Innovation is the key for success and to be ahead in market place. It is our desire that every one in our University innovate continuously; we want to see innovation in teaching and learning, innovation in research, innovation in administration and innovation in extension work. For example, if a student wants to get something, he has to go to finance officer, he has to go to registrar, he has to go to library or for various other things. This year we have introduced a single window system for students. If he hands over a paper in one place, they will take care of all other things. He need not go from window to window. And innovation of extension work, I found today's news paper, for the first time probably (nobody has attempted this) we want to introduce robots to our school students which I saw which is happening in Germany. I thought that it should be introduced in our own country. Where we have lots of youngsters, crores and crores of youngsters and we are starting our extension work. One of the innovation and extension work we will be training the school students for introducing robot system technology.

The recent survey, reports that, India has recently introduced Global Innovation Index called GII. Our score is 3.5 and India is ranked 23 among 107 countries. Even though we are above China which is ranked as 29. UAE is ranked 14th with global innovation index of 3.1. This should be a concern to us. US stands in No. 1 spot in innovation index of 5.8. India having the maximum young population in the world and being rated in the country is the highest intellectual capability and if it is rated 23rd, it is not an achievement at all. In this, the educational institutions, I feel have a major role to play. Unless we cultivate innovative culture in our institutions, India cannot have better global innovation index. When I speak of innovation, I am reminded of the writings of US futurologist Raw Kurzweil. He said, in the first 20 years of 20th century, we saw more advancement than in all the 19th century put together and we want experience 100 years of progress in the 21st century, it will more like 20,000 years of progress at the current rate. That's how the world is growing, India is growing. We have to be part of globe. It is US counsel on competitiveness declared about US. It is applicable to us also. Innovation is the single most important factor in determining America's success in 21st century. I think it is applicable to us also. That is why; number of countries, developing countries as well as developed countries are concentrating on Research and Development. For example, since late 1990's, China has boosted its Research and Developments spending by 50% and recently, under the newly elected president for second time, Mr. Yu. Zinto, Baiging wants to raise this amount up to 2.5% of GDP that is they will be spending 115 billion US dollars annually for Research and Developments alone. This is a very good example of a huge developing country. Take for example a poor country like Ethiopia, one of the poorest countries of the world, is committed to bringing a broad band connection within the reach of all its 74 million population by 2007. This shows that even poor countries, they would like to innovate, they would like to have the modern development and India cannot lack behind.

As I told you, our dream is that, one day, India will lead the world in higher education. For that all of us, all the educational institutions in the country must have a clear vision with correct value and attempt to attain the same by nurturing innovative culture.

Organizational Core Values and How They Work

D. AMARCHAND

An organizational value is "a belief that a specific mode of conduct is preferable to an opposite or different mode of conduct "(Milton Rokeach, 1973 Nature of Human Values). Some organizations think of their values as their "guiding beacon" or "ideals" directing the process of organizational development and growth. Others describe them as the components of their organizational philosophy. They do relate how organizations deal with their beliefs about people and work. They also define non-negotiable behaviours. More and more studies show that successful companies place a great deal of emphasis on their values.

Values are also the essence of corporate culture because they set out the "do's and don'ts" in decision-making as well as behaviour. Living them or practicing is what matters. They are not made to be put on the wall and forgotten about!

Organizational Culture is a system of shared values about what is important, what behaviours are appropriate and about feelings and relationships internally and externally. Values and cultures need to be unique to the organization, widely shared and reflected in daily practice and relevant to the company purpose and strategy. But there is no single best culture.

(Consider the highest values which become the building blocks of some of the great religions). Though there are many values in an organizational situation, a few, (may be 5) become the core values and also the operative values. They must be symbolized by one or two words, then must have a clear definition in the organization's context, followed by defined behaviours. They support your vision, shape your culture and reflect what you value. Here are some examples to explain how the values work when practiced. The meaning is given first and some aspects of how it works are given next.

TEAMWORK

Listening to and respecting each other whilst working together to mutually beneficial results.

When we are not sure we check with others as to what they meant.

Every one has strength which we value and will use whenever possible

All team meetings will include a progress report from every one and requests for help when needed.

TEAMWORK (ANOTHER APPROACH)

Providing support to one another, working cooperatively, respecting one another's views and making our work environment fun and enjoyable.

We help others to achieve their deadlines without having to be asked.

All projects have identified points which are celebrated by the whole team.

We work with one another with enthusiasm and appreciation.

We work with one another without manipulation.

Conflict is resolved according to agreed guidelines for the particular team.

Honesty

Being open and honest in all our dealings and maintaining the highest integrity at all times. (Consider this example. US Public Law: Put loyalty to the highest moral principles and to the country before loyalty to persons, party or Government departments).

All concerns are aired constructively with solutions offered.

Each person is as skilled in some way as another and is entitled to express their views without interruptions.

Excellence

Always doing what we say we will and striving for excellence and quality in everything we do. (Remember subjective and objective quality-refer to Robert Pirsig, The Art of Motor Cycle Maintenance) Quality will always delight the client whilst staying within budget limitations.

If we give our word we keep it unless agreed otherwise by all the concerned parties.

Commitment

Working with urgency and commitment to be successful from individual and company perspectives. (Consider another US Public Law: Give a full day's labour for a full day's pay: giving earnest effort and best thought to the performance of duties).

Timeframes are always met unless urgent circumstances mean we have to renegotiate new time frames with all parties.

Accountability

We take the responsibility for our actions. No need to search for scapegoats or passing the buck.

We understand our customer and care for them. Our performance is responsible for any repeat business with our customers.

At every meeting with our customer we ask what we could have done better and implement best of their suggestions before we do them again.

All agreements are met. (My word is my promise!)

We know the job and do the work as professionals. Reliability and accountability go together.

Personal Development

We value learning, feedback, coaching and mentoring.

We all coach and mentor one another.

All our opportunities for own learning are pursured.

Whenever we undertake a new project it is our duty and responsibility to express our training needs and gather required skills.

A Digression: The values and the operative culture of our nation may be of equal interest in this context since the national as a whole can be also looked as an organization. Check for yourself the prevalence of values like Honesty, Trustworthiness, Self-regulation, Sense of Fairness, Self-respect, shame and guilt and the public sense of aesthetics and hygiene. Add the vision of our leader from the district level to the National level, of different parties, of different Heads of institutions. You will certainly get perplexed and will surely find an answer one day or the other. Let your search begin today itself, each one of the value presents a difficult question and we remain an underdeveloped country in the human development index.

Many of the companies focus on a "Big Idea" or a few key words that simply express what the purpose or values of the organization are, how the organization works and what it is like to work there. But the 'Big Idea' on its own isn't enough. To build commitment and drive improved performance it needs to be:

Understood across the organization
Integrated into relationships between stakeholders
Enduring and building on a legacy of past success
Habitual, with behaviours repeated collective and routine.

Organizational Values, Vision and Culture in Institutions of Higher Learning

H.R. VENKATESHA

Once India's huge population was seen as one of the biggest liability. In today's global environment our one billion plus population is one of the important strength of India. On the one hand, huge population provides wide market for goods and services marketed by national and multinational companies. On the other hand, in the background of ageing population in the developed countries English speaking, technology enabled, young, educated population with global mindset is an asset to countries like India.

Despite rapid advancement in knowledge economy, India is still seen as a non-competitive labour-oriented society. Two-thirds of our work force depend on agriculture for their living. The productivity of Indian agricultural labourer is one of the lowest in the world. There is over dependence on Agriculture.

Even though in most industrial sectors, competitive advantage is built around labour, productivity and efficiency of Indian industrial employees needs to be increased. In this background it is the responsibility of institutions of higher learning to prepare our youths for global competition in all sectors with specific focus on knowledge economy.

India needs large number of world class institutes of higher learning. At present, the world-class institutions are mainly limited to the Indian Institutes of Technology (IITs), the Indian Institutes of Management (IIMs) and perhaps a few others such as the All India Institute of Medical Sciences and the Tata Institute of Fundamental Research. (None of these institutions stands one in top ten in the world in their respective segments) These institutions, and good Universities (exceptionally few) combined, enroll well under 1 per cent of the student population. Without adequate higher education and research institutions providing a critical mass of skilled and educated people, no country can ensure genuine endogenous and sustainable development. In particular, developing countries like India cannot reduce the gap separating them from the industrially developed ones. Sharing knowledge, international co-operation and new technologies can offer new opportunities to reduce this gap. Higher education has given ample proof of its viability over the centuries and of its ability to change and to induce change and progress in society. Owing to the scope and pace of change, society has become increasingly knowledge-based so that higher learning and research now act as essential components of cultural, socio-economic and environmentally sustainable development of individuals, communities and nations.

CRITICAL FACTORS IN OVVC IN INSTITUTIONS OF HIGHER LEARNING

- India's main competitors—especially China but also Singapore, Taiwan, and South Korea—are investing in large and differentiated higher education systems. They are providing access to large number of students at the bottom of the academic system while at the same time building some research-based universities that are able to compete with the world's best institutions.

- The *London Times Higher Education Supplement* ranking of the world's top 200 universities included three in China, three in Hong Kong, three in South Korea, one in Taiwan, and one in India (an Indian Institute of Technology at number 4—the specific campus was not specified). These countries are positioning themselves for leadership in the knowledge-based economies of the coming era.
- India has significant advantages in the 21st century knowledge race. It has a large higher education sector—the third largest in the world in student numbers, after China and the United States. It uses English as a primary language of higher education and research. It has a long academic tradition. Academic freedom is respected. There are a small number of high quality institutions, departments, and centers that can create necessary momentum of quality improvement in higher education.
- It is not only students but also teachers who are at the receiving end of the ongoing transformation in higher education. The nation today witnesses the declining popularity of teaching as a profession, not only among the students that we produce, but also among parents, scientists, society and the government. The teaching profession today attracts only those who have missed all other "better" opportunities in life, and is increasingly mired in bureaucratic controls and anti-education concepts such as "hours" of teaching "load", "paid-by-the-hour", "contractual" teachers, etc. With privatization reducing education to a commodity, teachers are reduced to tutors and teaching is reduced to coaching. The consumerist boom and the growing salary differentials between teachers and other professionals and the value systems of the emerging free market economy have made teaching one of the least attractive professions that demands more work for less pay. There may be very few exceptions. Yet, the society expects teachers not only to be inspired but also to do an inspiring job!

HIGHER EDUCATION

The architect of Microsoft, Bill Gates once rightly commented: "There is no better investment for developing countries like India (and China) than investing in education". In this knowledge economy, educated population is a great asset to any nation. The potential for growth and development is enormous if over a billion people, one-sixth of humanity is educated, creative and enterprising. Malcolm Gills, the President of Rice University, USA, rightly commented: "Today, more than ever before in human history, the wealth—or poverty of nations depends on the quality of higher education. Those with a larger repertoire of skills and a greater capacity for learning can look forward to life times of unprecedented economic fulfilment. But in the coming decades the poorly educated face little better than the dreary prospects of lives of quiet desperation". In India the productivity of employees is a matter of concern. One of the reasons is quality of higher education. We have number, not the quality. Even in so called sun rise sector like Information technology, where India has an edge over other nations, some flag our vast pool of labour as an advantage while others say that a majority of them are not working in cutting edge areas. India has to create an environment that does not produce industrial workers and labourers but fosters knowledge workers. Such people must be at the cutting edge of knowledge, be competitive and innovative. Education development has a major role to play in shaping knowledge workers and, in turn, placing India in the vanguard in the information age.

Indian conditions in higher education are different from developed countries of the world. The world of education in India encompasses different 'worlds' that live side by side. One world includes only a fortunate few with access to modern institutions, computers, Internet access and expensive overseas education. A second world wants to maintain status quo—teachers, administrators, textbook publishers, students—all have reasons to prefer things to remain as they are or change only gradually. The third world struggles with fundamental issues such as no books, wrong books, teachers desperately in need of training, teachers with poor commitment, rote learning of irrelevant material, classrooms with un manageable number of students, dirty floors and no toilets. India cannot hope to succeed in the information age on the back of such three disparate worlds.

The imperative for India is to raise standards of the vast majority with poor education, break the education sector free from its inertia and forge a society that places knowledge as the cornerstone of its development.

In India higher education is faced with great challenges and difficulties related to financing, equity of conditions at access into and during the course of studies, staff development, skills-based training, enhancement and preservation of quality in teaching, research and services, relevance of Government controlled regulatory bodies, poor benchmarks as standards (where foreign universities are not allowed), lack of level playing field (with Government subsidies to very few organizations), relevance of programmes, and employability of graduates. At the same time, higher education is being challenged by new opportunities relating to technologies that are improving the ways in which knowledge can be produced, managed, disseminated, accessed and controlled. Equitable access to these technologies is a big challenge in countries like India.

Why Higher Education is Important?

- Only about 10 per cent of the total student population enters higher education in India, as compared to over 15 per cent in China and 50 per cent in the major industrialized countries. Opportunity of higher education to other deserving Indian youths would make India a super knowledge power house.
- World Development Report entitled "Knowledge for Development" significantly records that "Knowledge is like light, weightless and intangible; it can easily travel through the world, enlightening the lives of people everywhere. Yet billions of people still live in the darkness of poverty—unnecessarily". This is truer with India.
- With about 380 universities and deemed universities

(Knowledge commission recommends 1500 Universities), over 17,000 colleges and hundreds of national and regional research institutes, Indian higher education and research sector is the third largest in the world, in terms of the number of students it caters to. However, not a single Indian university finds even a mention in a recent international ranking of the top 200 universities of the world, except an IIT ranked at 41.

VISION FOR INSTITUTIONS OF HIGHER LEARNING

Webster's dictionary defines "vision" in two ways: first, "unusual discernment, foresight" or "imagination." And second, "the act or power of seeing." We must be adept at both. We must have the vision to see where higher education can take us in a future where both freedom and competition are on the move. This is a world defined less by where you live and more by what you know. We must take advantage. We must find a way to give all Indians the skills they'll need to lead in this new world. This will take all of the foresight and imagination we can muster. At the same time, we must see clearly—with no colored glasses—the conditions that lead to a well-educated citizenry right now. And we must hold ourselves accountable for providing them. Thus, the vision for education in India would be "to create a competitive, yet co-operative, knowledge-based society". (*Source*: Government of India, Policy Framework for Reforms in Education).

Strategic Objectives

Several strategic objectives would have to be pursued in order to realize this vision. They are:

- Provide quality primary education facilities to every citizen of India.
- Provide and support the private sector in the establishment of high quality secondary education facilities.
- Encourage the establishment of world class higher education facilities from Private, Government and NGOs.

- Encourage the creation of state-of-the-art professional research-based education institutions in all disciplines.
- Integrate education with information and communication technologies to:

    1. Create smart schools,
    2. Network and deliver education and training,
    3. Institutionalize distance education,
    4. Create and maintain data bases, and continuously analyze trends.

- Develop human resources required for the education process.
- Continuously upgrade educational content in multiple media.
- Create institutional linkages to other sectors of social development such as health and rural development.
- Motivate non-resident Indians to participate in India's education programmes on a voluntary or sabbatical basis.
- Market India as a destination for affordable, high quality education hub.

Guiding Principles

The following guiding principles must permeate the pursuit of the above strategic objectives:

- Foster a healthy mix of state supported education with private initiatives.
- Costs of education must be affordable to the under-privileged sections of society.
- Quality of education must be continuously monitored and upgraded to ensure high standards.
- User pays principle to be enforced strictly for higher education supported by loan schemes as well as financial grants for economically and socially backward sections of society.
- Privatization of higher education is need of the hour. Profit should not be treated as a dirty word in

education. Legalize profit in education sector. This makes corporate sector to enter education in a big way.

- Government subsidy for few Government institutions has to be reconsidered to give level playing field for both Government and Private institutions.

Diversification for Enhanced Equity of Opportunity

Diversifying higher education models and criteria is essential both to meet increasing international demand and to provide access to various delivery modes and to extend access to an ever-wider public, in a lifelong perspective, based on flexible entry and exit points to and from the system of higher education. Diversification brings in enhanced equity of opportunity. More diversified systems of higher education are characterized by new types of tertiary institutions: public, private and non-profit institutions, amongst others. Institutions should be able to offer a wide variety of education and training opportunities: traditional degrees, short courses, part-time study, flexible schedules, modularized courses, supported learning at a distance, etc.

Innovative Educational Approaches: Critical Thinking and Creativity

In a world undergoing rapid changes, there is a perceived need for a new vision and paradigm of higher education, which should be student-oriented, calling for in-depth reforms and an open access policy so as to cater for ever more diversified categories of people, and of its contents, methods, practices and means of delivery, based on new types of links and partnerships with the community and with the broadest sectors of society. Higher education institutions should educate students to become well informed and deeply motivated citizens, who can think critically, analyze problems of society, look for solutions to the problems of society, apply them and accept social responsibilities. To achieve these goals, it may be necessary to recast curricula, using new and appropriate methods, so as to go beyond cognitive mastery of disciplines. New pedagogical and didactical approaches should be accessible and promoted in order to facilitate the acquisition of skills, competences and abilities for communication, creative and critical analysis, independent thinking and team work in multicultural contexts, where creativity also involves combining traditional or local knowledge and know-how with advanced science and technology. These recast curricula should take into account the gender dimension and the specific cultural, historic and economic context of the country. Academic personnel should play a significant role in determining the curriculum. New methods of education will also imply new types of teaching-learning materials. These have to be coupled with new methods of evaluation that will promote not only powers of memory but also powers of comprehension, skills for practical work and creativity.

Higher Education Personnel and Students as Major Actors

A vigorous policy of staff development is an essential element for higher education institutions. Clear policies should be established concerning higher education teachers, who nowadays need to focus on teaching students how to learn and how to take initiatives rather than being exclusively founts of knowledge. To this end, more importance should be attached to international experience. This should include student involvement in issues that affect that level of education, in evaluation, the renovation of teaching methods and curricula and, in the institutional framework in force, in policy-formulation and institutional management. As students have the right to organize and represent themselves, students' involvement in these issues should be guaranteed. Furthermore, in view of the role of higher education for lifelong learning, experience outside the institutions ought to be considered as a relevant qualification for higher educational staff. Clear policies should be established by all higher education institutions preparing teachers of early childhood education and for primary and secondary schools, providing stimulus for constant innovation in curriculum, best practices in teaching methods and familiarity with diverse learning styles. It is vital to have appropriately trained administrative and technical personnel.

Total Quality Management in Institutions of Higher Learning

The philosophy of Total Quality Management (TQM) has its relevance in educational institutions too. It is application of management techniques for continuous quality improvement (CQI) in the academia with appropriate tools for meeting the needs and expectations of the stakeholders. The TQM approach in educational institutions emphasizes that the institute should have a vision of what it wants to be and clearly define its mission compatible with the vision, and accordingly lay down its objectives to be transformed into specific, attainable, meaningful goals. Many institutions in the realm of higher education lack the courage and commitment to implement TQM.

Quality in higher education is a multi-dimensional concept, which should embrace all its functions, and activities: teaching and academic programmes, research and scholarship, staffing, students, buildings, facilities, equipment, services to the community and the academic environment. Internal self-evaluation and external review, conducted openly by independent specialists, are vital for enhancing quality. Independent national bodies should be established and comparative standards of quality, recognized at international level, should be defined. Due attention should be paid to specific institutional, national and regional contexts in order to take into account diversity and to avoid uniformity. Stakeholders should be an integral part of the institutional evaluation process.

Quality also requires that higher education should be characterized by its international dimension: exchange of knowledge, interactive networking, mobility of teachers and students, and international research projects, while taking into account the national cultural values and circumstances.

To attain and sustain national, regional or international quality, certain components are particularly relevant, notably careful selection of staff and continuous staff development, in particular through the promotion of appropriate programmes for academic staff development, including teaching/learning methodology and mobility between countries, between higher education institutions, and between higher education institutions and the world of work, as well as student mobility within and between countries. The information technologies are an important tool in this process, owing to their impact on the acquisition of knowledge and know-how.

The Potential and the Challenge of Technology

The rapid breakthroughs in new information and communication technologies have changed the way knowledge is developed, acquired and delivered. It is also important to note that the new technologies offer opportunities to innovate on course content and teaching methods and to widen access to higher learning. However, it should be borne in mind that new information technology does not reduce the need for teachers but changes their role in relation to the learning process and that the continuous dialogue that converts information into knowledge and understanding becomes fundamental. Higher education institutions should lead in drawing on the advantages and potential of new information and communication technologies, ensuring quality and maintaining high standards for education practices and outcomes in a spirit of openness, equity and international co-operation.

Strengthening Higher Education Management and Financing

The management and financing of higher education require the development of appropriate planning and policy-analysis capacities and strategies, based on partnerships established between higher education institutions and state and national planning and co-ordination bodies, so as to secure appropriately streamlined management and the cost-effective use of resources. Higher education institutions should adopt forward-looking management practices that respond to the needs of their environments. Managers in higher education must be responsive, competent and able to evaluate regularly, by internal and external mechanisms, the effectiveness of procedures and administrative rules.

The ultimate goal of management should be to enhance the institutional mission by ensuring high-quality teaching, training and research, and services to the community. This objective requires governance that combines social vision, including understanding of global issues, with efficient managerial skills. Leadership in higher education is thus a major social responsibility and can be significantly strengthened through dialogue with all stakeholders, especially teachers and students, in higher education. The participation of teaching faculty in the governing bodies of higher education institutions should be taken into account, within the framework of current institutional arrangements, bearing in mind the need to keep the size of these bodies within reasonable bounds.

Vision for Higher Education

- Innovation will be at the heart of competitiveness in the information society. Innovation is a commitment to create future growth. Societies will tend to be research-intensive. Already, R&D expenditures are 1.8% of GDP in Europe, 2.7% in USA and 2.8% in Japan and would tend to move higher in absolute and relative terms. In India it is less than 1% of GDP. This has to be addressed. Tighter patent laws will support the sustenance of such expenditures. Innovation without knowledge and people is unimaginable.
- The 21st Century witnessed the global economy changing fast where knowledge substitutes mere physical capital as the fundamental source of wealth. India should have proper vision to develop as a super knowledge power.
- In keeping with the Universal Declaration of Human Rights, admission to higher education should be based on the merit, capacity, efforts, perseverance and devotion, showed by those seeking access to it, and can take place in a lifelong scheme, at any time, with due recognition of previously acquired skills. In Indian scenario special efforts have to be made to accommodate deserving students from economically and socially deprived sections.

VALUES IN INSTITUTIONS OF HIGHER LEARNING

Performance of an institution of higher learning should not

be seen merely in terms of value-addition but also in terms of values addition. Values in institutions of higher learning are culmination of the values professed in society, teachers, management and students. For example, to a true scholar the joy of learning is the highest reward and an end in itself. Sharing this with other scholars and students, and through sharing creating love for learning in them, is a basic value of academic life. Essential values for an academician in pursuit of knowledge are intellectual freedom, honesty, responsibility and intellectual humility. Progress of ideals is not possible without the freedom of intellect to explore the unexplored.

Providing high quality education to the youth of society is the main aim of an Institution of higher learning. The main aim of the teaching-learning process is to create love for learning in the learner, encourage and nourish his/her curiosity and to guide him/her in the hopeful exploration of the world of knowledge. It is the intellectual training and development of right attitudes which are important rather than information transmission. Therefore, the highest value should attach to the educational injunction "teach your pupils to think". While evaluating students' higher levels of academic competence—comprehension, analysis, synthesis, evaluation and judgment are to be tested.

Some important values which need special emphasis in the administration of higher learning are creation of effective channels of consultation and upward flow of ideas, monitoring and evaluation of the work done by teachers, academic departments and other staff, and a system for demanding accountability from academic and administrative authorities.

The academic life of an Institution of higher learning is a small sub-system of the larger social system. The values of the sub-system are naturally affected by those prevalent in the larger system. Students, teachers and other staff, bring to their work place some of the negative values of today's Indian society, like caste prejudices, greater concern for filial connections than for propriety and fair play, less than respectful attitude towards women, and overwhelming concern for rights and hardly any for duties. Power and position are viewed as rewards meant for enjoyment rather than burdens of responsibility. Upholding values in academic life has admittedly become difficult in this hostile value climate of the external society. Many have developed cynical attitudes and give it up as a hopeless task.

It is frequently argued that values cannot be 'taught' in the classroom; they can only be 'caught' from the environment. The argument is true only to a limited extent. Any body of knowledge which has a rational basis and a reasonably coherent, conceptual framework can be taught in the classroom. Yet it would be catastrophic to accept the defeatist stance that the values of academic life cannot be improved unless those of the larger society improve. The only source of hope for facing the present values crisis is the knowledge, wisdom and strength of character of the learned academics in the institutes of higher learning. These seats of learning should not become passive, value-neutral institutions, merely swaying in the hostile value winds blowing in the society. They have to become active value generating sources for not only holding academic ideals but also those by which the society ought to be regulated. This has been the role of the learned teachers' right since the ancient times in our country. The challenges of this responsibility must be accepted so that the institutions of higher learning become active changing agents for transforming the value system of the society as a hole.

Take Care of the 'Value' Generators

- The regulatory approaches need urgent change with more peer review driven mechanisms rather than the current bureaucratic model.
- The approach of the Government has to change from controller to developer and facilitator.
- Addressing the issues of equity and excellence simultaneously will remain crucial to ensure inclusive strategies.
- The 'craft' of teaching goes more with the knowledge, attitude, culture and value a teacher professes. This has to be given importance in Recruitment and Faculty development programs
- Reforms in higher education would reduce bureaucratic controls, attract better talent, provide

more operational freedom, improve transparency, increase accountability, remove corruption, encourage self-financing, and to reward productivity and punish laxity.

ROLE OF CULTURE IN INSTITUTIONS OF HIGHER LEARNING

World class universities require world class professors and students—and a culture to sustain and stimulate them. An institution of higher learning's culture consists of institutional characteristics such as size and location, curricular structure and academic standards, student-faculty relationships, student characteristics, faculty characteristics, the physical environment and the vision and mission of the Institution. It is the underlying assumptions about how all these characteristics relate which actually constitutes Institution's culture. Cultures, however, often exists within sub-cultures. The culture of the Institution would be considered strong if there exists a high degree of congruence among the sub-cultures. Cultural strength can be either an asset or a liability. It can lead to lack of innovation and groupthink or to innovation and creativity.

Leadership and Cultural Change

Cultural change doesn't come easily, especially when shared assumptions are firmly established. However, new cultures are created and even changed under strong leadership. Cultural change is more easily attained in new institutional settings but the challenge is great when assumptions have been held for a long time. This is one of the biggest challenges in India. Change is likely to be highly resisted because many faculty members are motivated by power which is derived from status in the academic marketplace. Unless there is change in the entire higher education system or at least in a substantial number of institutions, faculty members will be reluctant to change.

- Education is too important and too demanding to leave it alone to Government. All types of

Management and Ownership models like Private, NGOs, philanthropic, and religious institutions have to be allowed to enter education sector in a big way. Even companies and firms for profit should be allowed to operate.

- Industry in-house departments should be allowed to give degrees. This has to be encouraged more in Engineering, Information Technology, Media and Management disciplines.
- There is shortage of quality teachers in most of the disciplines. This has to be addressed by offering compensation in par with industry.
- Foreign Universities have to be encouraged to operate in India. This helps to set in new standards. Competition would definitely offer better options for students.
- FDI should be allowed in Higher Education. This brings in necessary resources to strengthen the infrastructures necessary for higher education.
- Credible Independent Accreditation bodies have to be encouraged to make students and parents choose right Institute and/or University of higher learning. Otherwise mushroom growth of Universities and Institutions may take students, parents and system for a ride. For example, in Chhattisgarh, where over 150 private universities and colleges came up within a couple of months, till the scam got exposed by a public interest litigation and the courts ordered the state government in 2004 to derecognize and close most of these universities or merge them with the remaining recognized ones.
- A clearly differentiated academic system has not been created in India—a system where there are some clearly identified institutions that receive significantly greater resources than Universities and Institutes in general. This can be linked to the strength and performance of an institution.
- Research demands huge long-term investment. There is 'risk' regarding guaranteed return on investment. This has to be addressed immediately. FDI, Foreign

universities and more freedom for private players would help to increase investment in R&D.

- India should move from 'brain drain' to 'brain gain'. Throughout the developed world, especially in USA good number of academicians and researchers in Institutions of higher learning are people of Indian origin. They have to be attracted back to India. In addition to this brain gain, if possible the best possible brains from different parts of the world are to be attracted to India. Thanks to liberalization, the opinion about India is changing for better in the global scenario.
- Institutions of higher learning have to calculate 'human equity'. This has to be regularly audited and should be projected as strength of an Institution.

Building a World Class Organisation

MOHAMMED GALIB HUSSAIN

The growth and development of any business organization originates in the vision of its promotor. The vision and methods of translating the vision into practice of some of the excellent Indian organisations are discussed below:

VISION AND ACTION

S.M. Datta's Hindustan Unilever Ltd's vision has been touching lives across the length and breath of the country and to make its brand a household name. HUL touches lives not only through manufacturing and marketing but through building enduring relationships. Its strength lies in its relationship with consumers, employees, shareholders, dealers and distributors. Management techniques may change and technologies become obsolete. It is its relationship that remains enduring.

Rahul Bajaj's long-term vision is to build a world class two-wheeler manufacturing. To do so Bajaj Auto has to:

- Improve its product quality.
- Expand its market.
- Improve its quality standards to meet international standards.

Therefore in line with its vision, Bajaj Auto is improving its quality by massive investment in R and D, to gain technologies entering into foreign collaboration and understanding value engineering. To expand market it enters into mergers and consolidations. It has set-up manufacturing facilities in several foreign countries.

Ratan Tata's vision has always been to "constantly on the move and in keeping with the changing times". Ratan Tata always wanted to be the first truly Indian car manufacturer. To transformer his vision into action, he has gone in for major restructuring in the organization like introducing the latest and the best technologies. Telco always keeps its costs down.

Parvinder Singh's vision is to "make the presence of Ranbaxy felt in the world market". The following steps have been taken to turn the vision into reality:

- To demonstrate commitment and involvement in quality.
- To empower employees by involving them in the core processes.
- To reorganize and have global bases.
- To reduce the number of levels within the organization.
- To shift in the attitude of people towards more innovation.
- To have the same quality levels for the imports and exports.

Dhirubhai Ambani's vision can be put into simple terms thus:

- To operate the country's largest petroleum refinery.
- To be globally number one are in the manufacture of PET (Polyethylene terephthalate).
- Lead the world in the integrated manufacturing value chain from the naphtha to textiles.

To convert the vision into action Dhirubhai Ambani took the following steps:

- Disallow hierarchical structures to be created, preferring teams to manage.
- Creation of five high-powered committees to oversee global business, domestic business, finance, pricing and compensation.

PERSONAL PROFILES OF SOME VISIONARIES

Adi Burzorji Godrej

It was his parsi mother who shaped the personality of her son. When he was four years old, his mother encouraged him to get rid off his timidity and threw him in the street to watch roadside monkey show. He was put on a monthly allowance of Rs. 75 when he was just 10 years old and was asked to take care of school fees, books and clothes within the amount. At the age of 13 his mother encouraged him to travel around the country.

Godrej manages around thirty companies not through operational control but through his vision. He has trained himself to manage these companies through meetings. He avoids pleasantries and inconsequential exchanges, with his notes in the right hand; he controls the tempo of meeting and reaches to the core of the issue. He is fond of saying, "I am never in a situation when I am over whelmed with work". He manages overseas operations through a predetermined video-conferencing. As a performance review, he holds three-hour meeting once a year with each of his reporting managers.

Godrej strictly follows empowerment systematically pushing both decision-making and control down the line. Even of the cost of his own judgment, he maintains the ethos of empowerment. In his empowered corporation, Godrej now plays the role of felicitator.

He describes his life's motto as "change organize and learn". It would be difficult to find another CEO so well informed not only about his business but also about his environment and international affairs. He learns from research reports, newspapers, management books and net. He gathers and memorises facts such as gross domestic product, per capital income of various countries with which he has to deal. He spares a month in every year attending training programme and seminars. He uses the knowledge for changing business practices in his companies as well as changing himself.

Dynamic by nature he does not need much time to reach to the core of the issue. He goes about management change process very fast.

He is basically an introvert and had problems in redesigning his organization and empowerment was difficult for him. After all empowerment involves interaction with his colleagues which is a difficult task for introvert. He overcame this deficiency by managing himself.

THEORY OF VISION

From the foregone discussion, it should be clear that every promotor of a world class organization filled with a vision which fires his imagination and he in turn translates into action by firing the imagination of his colleagues with his vision.

This part of the paper addresses the question of the origin of vision.

Vision is a crystallized long-term goal of what can and should be achieved. It stimulates people to new levels of commitment and enthusiasm. Shares beliefs and values are integrated leading to change in the culture of the organization. Fired with vision, the members of the organization come out of their narrow domain and focus on a broader organizational perspective. In the first place, how do these transformational leaders get vision? What is the source of vision?

Vision: An Insight from Hindu Mythology

There are two occasions on which a female vedanti defeats a male vedanti in the matter of argumentation. One such occasion was a debute on the question of visibility of god.

Garge, a lady vedanti argued with textual, logical and reasoning support from Vedas and proved that it was beyond the reach of a human being to see god with his naked eyes. Audience in the debate were convinced that Garge was right in her contention. The judges were about to declare her the winner.

A Gnostic among the audience got up and put forth a claim that stunned every one among the audience as well as the judges. The claim was that he could make all the people in the *sabha* to see god within term minutes. The judges permitted him to prove his claim.

He started describing god in his poetic frenziness and within no time everyone started seeing god with naked eyes. This is the power of Gnostic's third eye. A Gnostic not only visualizes what cannot be visualized by others but also makes others see as if has physical existence. Where from the mystic gets knowledge? It is pure intuition according to theology. This is the stage in which a visionary drops all modes of thought, reasoning, logic, memory, and emotions. It is pure intelligence in the terminology of philosophers. It is beyond proof; beyond empirical evidence; beyond physical existence, above logic. It is not thinking because thinking repeats itself. One thinks when he is not intuitive. Bankruptcy of intuition leads to thinking, logic, reasoning and emotions. To be a visionary is to be intuitive.

MANAGEMENT BY FAITH

From the above discussion, the reader must have noted a transformational leader is driven by strong faith or trust. Faith is a term used by theologists and trust is used by behavioural scientists.

The Holy Quran, a revealed book to mankind, emphasizes the role of faith in organizational life. Only people infused with faith will be successful. According to Quran, through faith a finite human being gets closer to infinite god and gains immeasurable strength to do those things which can not be imagined by an ordinary human being. With faith a powerless human being gets the endless power by his proximity to God. The Holy Quran says:

> Time itself is witness! Verily, man is in loss; excepting those who have faith and strive righteously; offerwise counsel and are models of perseverance and patience.
>
> *(103:1-3, Quran)*

From the development of formal theories of management till today the question that props up again and again is: what is an effective system of management? Depending upon their socio-cultural context as well as socio-political context, management theorists have tried to give different solutions to this problem. These include Management by exception, Management by crisis, Management by results, Management by objectives, Management by Communication, Management by participation, Management by motivation and so on. These are all the contributions of western management thinkers.

In India, S.K. Chakraborthy[1] developed a creative concept called Management by values and R.S. Dwivedi[2] contributed Management by trust.

It is an effective management device based on trusting behaviour of all the members of the Organization. Trusting behaviour is authentic, genuine, development facilitative and supportive.

It increases an individual's sense of trust in oneself and in other in such a way that others reciprocate.

Management by trust leads to optimization of organizational structures and of organizational process, i.e. decision-making, communication, control and leadership trusting behaviour leads to conflict resolution in such a way that paves the way towards constructive outcomes. Faith leads to integration of individual, group and organizational goals. Modern organization theorists like McGregor, Argyris and Likert advocate trusting behaviour for optimizing organizational structure.

DO NOT FOCUS ON CORE COMPETENCIES

The concept of core competencies is very beautifully brought out in the following story from Ramayana.

Sampati, a vulture, after narrating his story to the monkeys said, "On the peak of Tirukut Hill stands the city of Lanka. In the Ashoka Garden, Sita, sits in grief and mighty Ravana lives in Lanka. I am able to see what you do not see for a vulture's sight is unlimited. I am old, or else I would have helped you in my own humble way."

"I can leap across 800 mile salt sea out somehow I am not confident of coming back", said Angad. The bears interjected, "How can we let go you are our king", Angad turned towards Hanuman, "Oh Mighty Hanuman' why are you keeping mum? You are a son of wind-god. You are intelligent and full of wisdom. There is nothing impossible for you to achieve. You alone can bring Sita and destroy mighty Ravana."

Hanuman becomes emotional and grows to the size of a mountain. He said, "I can leap across the salt ocean and after killing Ravana, I will wipeout his army".

The Story brings out the core competencies of vulture and monkey. Ability to see what can not be seen by others is the ability of a vulture. Leaping across is the competency of a monkey.

The concept of core competency is very well articulated by the economists in their comparative cost theory. According to the theory, a country should produce and export only those products and services in which has cost advantage.

In Business Management, the theory of core competency of corporations has been popularized by Prahalad and Hamel.[3] Core competencies refer to collective learning in the organization especially how to coordinate diverse production skills and integrate multiple streams of technologies. Sony's capacity of miniature or Philips optical-media expertise is core competencies of these companies. Honda has core competency in engines and power trains. It uses this competitive advantage in the production of two-wheelers, cars and generators.

In India many companies have moved away from core competencies and diversified into unrelated fields. There are strong reasons for not confining to core expertise in Indian context.

Growth demands that a corporation should move out of core area of business. In a growing economy sticking to your knitting means when the business matures, it leads to stagnation of growth. If it continues in the same business, its growth gets stifled.

To survive competition, Indian Inc believes that big is safe. To add to muscle and size, the companies are willing to take the risk of entering strategically dissimilar industry.

To use Management skill competitive advantage, HR as competitive advantage, corporations are entering into unrelated business.

To benefit from arbitrage, companies are venturing into sunrise sectors. They build and develop a new business and sell the business later for a profit.

Ambanis have entered into totally unrelated businesses such as iron ore, detergents, mining, telecommunications, energy and retail. Mahindras manage automobile manufacturing, hotels and host of other unrelated businesses. Eicher group is moving from engineering to shoes and garments. Aravind Mills produce textiles, telecommunications.

Tatas foray into telecommunications, steel, automobiles, tea and host of other businesses amply proves that to build a world class business corporation, a company need not stick to the knitting's as is popularly believed.

MANAGING CHANGE CREATIVELY

Today's organisations are in a state of flux. Management philosophy and practices are undergoing drastic change. Traditional resource-based organizations are maturing to knowledge-based organizations. Globalization, information technology, quality and diversity and ethics have changed the landscape of organizations.

How to Manage Change?

Psychology provides as three-step process of successful implementation of a change: unfreezing, changing and refreezing. Discarding old ideal and practices to learn new ideas and practices is unfreezing. Learning change involves mastering new ideal and practices. The Manager is required to help organizational embers, think reason and perform in new ways. In refreezing, organizational members accept new ideas and practices intellectually embrace them emotionally and assimilate them in their job life. This step aims at successful on the job practice rather than knowing a new procedure.

Change in Practice in Indian Organisations

The following examples illustrate now some of the top Indian organisations brought about change.

1. *Hindustan Unilever Ltd.*

HUL, consumer products giant, is the country's largest transnational company. It quickly seized upon opportunities of liberalization and started preparing to meet the challenges of keeping up its growth orientation in Indian market consolidating the group structure, realigning business, buying up competitors (like Tomco, Kwality and Milk Food), and cutting away layers, has resulted in a group which is means and lean in its outlook. Mergers and acquisition have been taken up on massive scale. Quest merged with Ponds and Lipton with Brooke Bond.

2. *Philps India Ltd.*

This Company has been restructured for operational efficiency. Four divisions are created, viz., consumer electronics, lighting electronic components and professional products and services. Non-remunerative units such as batteries and domestic appliance product lines were closed. To streamline operations, unique Data Ware Systems and Consultants Ltd., a subsidiary, was spin off as a separate unit. The Workforce was drastically reduced, the dealer network was expanded to cover every town with a population of 20 thousand and the number of service central was increased to 120 nation-wide. Restructuring was done by reducing three levels of management. Presently, the departmental heads report directly the industrial manager.

3. *The Kirloskar Group*

The 27 Companies which form the Kirloskar group have been restructured under seven inter-related business groups: fluid handling and compressor systems, electrical power equipment, prime movers and transmitters, metal cutting technologies, metal processing, project and system engineering and services. The restructuring forms a part of the strategic plan drawn by the group.

Behavioural Techniques and Change Management

Currently Indian Corporations are attempting to reach to the world class positions by employing the following behavioural techniques. They are improving the communication process, Management by values and using empowering leadership.

1. Improving Communication Process

During Post-liberalization, Indian Organisations have improved communication systems to enhance their effectiveness. Cemindia, Philips, IFCI and several other companies hold a daily meeting of their general managers and executive directors. Philips bridged the gap between the management and employers by sharing information regarding sales, profits and stocks.

At Cemindia, Pradeep Kapoor has accomplished a turnaround through an innovative management communication system. He keeps in touch with area chiefs every day; once in a month four chiefs meet him personally. He spends two or three days with the departmental heads providing a fillip to middle level managers.

2. Management by Values

Managing change requires, changing the values of the corporations. The tasks of the leaders are to get everyone live with these values by communicating them and recording those who follow them. Several Indian Organisations have started Managing by values. Infosys, NIL, SRF, Cemindia, IA, Philips, NICCO, IFCI, etc.

Values stressed by Infosys are:

> Transparency, teamwork, innovation, dedication to customers, respect for individuals. As N.R. Naryana Murthy points out: "Infosys used transparency as its mantra. Its annual report adopts the SEC disclosure norms as model strategic decisions are taken by a Management council consisting of core operational heads."

National Instruments Ltd manages itself on the basis of

core values such as transparency, honesty and innovation. At NICCO Corporation Ltd., the Chairman developed teamwork as a core value.

IFCI, STC, IA and Phillips also focus on transparency. Teamwork forms a crucial value at SRF, IFCI, IA and Cemindia. Customer orientation is becoming the core value at Onida.

3. *Empowering Leadership*

Empowering leadership is the process of unleashing and releasing potentials of people in the organization. This requires trust in people and their vast potentials. It is a process of delegating authority and resources to people enabling them to perform their work by making all decisions pertaining to it without seeking prior approval. Outstanding examples are Rahul Bajaj, Mukesh, Anil, Keshab Mahindra, Narayana Murthy, etc.

Coping up Change—India Inc.

In addition to the use of general measures of structural redesign and behavioural techniques, Indian corporations used a set of contingency techniques to cope up with change. These approaches can be illustrated by describing what has been done to manage change creatively by some of the following Organisations:

1. *Mahindra and Mahindra Ltd.*

In response to the changed situation it

- Restructured itself from traditional line to SBUs.
- Initiated business process reengineering.
- Collaborated with Ford for foray into the passenger car market.

2. *Birla Group*

Aditya Birla devised the following approach to manage changes in the business environment;

- Analyzing the management by clearly defining the authority and responsibilities of all senior managers.

- Evolving a six-point programme embracing participative management, knowledge integration programme, skill development programme system perfection, delegation and decentralization of authority and human resource development.
- Formulating a system in which the entire group exchanged knowledge, experiences, ideas, new processes, etc. Various committees have been formed to look after stores, sales, labour quality and finance.

PUTTING EMPLOYEES AND CUSTOMERS FIRST

Waterman[4] observes that excellent corporations are not created by exclusive reliance an technology or a bright idea or strategic asset obtained in these corporations. Corporations at the new frontier of excellence organize around their employees, empower employees give them some thing to believe in, challenge them and recognize them. They are committed to total customer relations, stress on quality of products and services and respond to customer needs.

Indian companies are gradually recognizing the significance of putting people first to accomplish corporate excellence. The following are the examples:

1. ITC Ltd.

The best kept secret of ITC is the quality and management of its human resource. The commitment of people in ITC is born out of knowledge. The Company has spent enormous time and money to build its people, it has evolved integrated training and development plans for each business area to transform the acquired knowledge into superior practice.

ITC is well known for its product quality. It produces the best products in the Industry. It spends a lot of money on product quality improvement.

2. Hindustan Unilever Ltd.

HUL adheres to the best marketing practices by following these steps:

- Validate every marketing step through customer feedback.
- Identify specific business needs for every new product.
- Judge advertising quality against specific parameters.
- Depend on market research to fine tune communication strategy.

3. TELCO

At Telco, the employees are given scholarship for higher education. The employees are motivated by highlighting their achievements in in-house journals. Ratan Tata believes in a well-knit family rather than simply a wage-structured organization.

4. BPL

Quality is the first priority of BPL. The Company has always stressed on quality due to which it has become an undisputed leader in consumer durable. To maintain the best quality, the following techniques are used:

- Measure customer satisfaction levels to generate ideas.
- Obtain feedback on new features from after-sales service team.
- Control quality by manufacturing components in-house.
- Modify technology to match local conditions and consumer requirements.

Notes and References

1. Chakraborty, S.K., Management by Values, Delhi: Oxford University Press, 1995.
2. Dwivedi, R.S., "Management by Trust: A Conceptual Model", *Group and Organization Studies*, 8(4) 1983, 375-405.
3. Prahalad, C.K and G. Hamel, "The Core Competence of Corporation", *Harvard Business Review*, May-June 1990.
4. Waterman, R.H., Frontiers of Excellence: Learning from Companies that put people first, London: Nicholas Brealey Publishing, 1994, 15-18.

PART II

Organizational Culture Dialectics : A Periscopic View

Creating a Conscious Organizational Culture

R. PADMAJA

Originally an anthropological term, culture refers to the underlying values, beliefs and code of practice that makes a community what it is.

Organizations are only one constituent element of society. People enter them from the surrounding community and bring their culture with them. It is still possible for organizations to have cultures of their own, as they possess the paradoxical quality of being 'part' of and 'apart' from society. Deal and Kennedy (1982) argue that culture is the single most important factor accounting for success or failure in organizations.

Culture has long been on the agenda of management theorists. Culture must mean changing the corporate ethos, the images and values that inform action and this new way of understanding organizational life must be brought into management process.

Cultures are classified into,

- Role cultures—are highly formalized, bound with regulations and paper work and authority and hierarchy dominate relations.
- Task cultures—they preserve a strong sense of basic mission of the organization and team work is the basis on which the jobs are designed.
- Power cultures—have a single power source, which may be an individual are a corporate group, control of rewards is a major source of power.

Handy points out that these types are usually tide to a particular structure and design of organization. A role culture has a typical pyramid structure. A task has a flexible matrix structures. A power culture has weblike communication structure.

MANAGING CULTURE

Corporate culture is really a kind of image for the company which top management would like to project. The image of the organization differs according to where you view it. Even in company with strong culture the social distance between the senior management and shop floor reality can be very wide. Cultures are hardly planned or predictable, they are the natural products of the social interaction and evolve and emerge overtime. Wilmott [1993] has fashioned a tuff challenge to what he calls corporate culturalism. This is the tendency for culture to be promoted as device for increasing corporate effectiveness.

Culture spans the range of management thinking and organizational culture has been one of the most enduring buzzwords of popular management. Organizational cultural will reduce work stress.

WORK STRESS AND ROLE OF MANAGERS

Work stress is recognized world-wide as a major challenge to workers' health and healthiness of their organizations. Stress at work can be a real problem to the organization as well as for its workers. Good management is the best form of stress prevention.

The culture of an organization is routinely created from the verbal and non-verbal messages expressed by the manager and leadership team about how people are expected to behave, what is important, what is valued, and what people have to do to fit in and be rewarded. Therefore, manager is the single greatest potential influence on the organizational culture.

ORGANIZATIONAL ROLE CULTURE

Role cultures are highly formalized, bound with regulations and paper work and authority and hierarchy dominate relations which are the major causes of stress. Managers play a vital role in maintaining organizational role culture for the effective management of the organization.

Stress at work is a real problem to the organization as well as its workers. Good management and good work organization are the best forms of stress preventions. If employees are already stressed, their managers should be aware of it and know how to help.

ORGANIZATIONAL ROLE STRESSES

Many things can cause stress. There are two broad categories; organizational stressors and life stressors. Organizational stressors are various factors in the work place that can cause stress.

Four general organizational stressors are task demands, working conditions, role demands, role conflict and role ambiguity, and interpersonal demands.

Task Demands

Task demand stressor is otherwise called work over load. At times individuals may find the work assigned to them to be too much to be carried out properly, such feelings can be said to be a form of stress. It can be caused due to lack of time, not able to cope with the demands or work itself may be beyond their capacity to perform. In case of too many activities it is referred to as qualitative overload. Some individuals do not appreciate a simplification or their jobs and continue their complex tasks which also results in sole overload.

Role Stagnation

Many people experience the frightening feeling of being fixed in their role within the organization. Most threatening is monotonous work, or work lacking in challenge, whereby time seems to stand still. As a result, some people develop a strong aversion to their jobs in their position.

Under Participation

Under participation is a feeling when an employee finds that his opinions are not sought in organizational problems, employee considers himself to be incompetent and irrelevant, and thinks that all his abilities are of no use for the organization. The development of this attitudes leads to stress.

Inadequacy of Role Authority

It means powerlessness, i.e. authority without power is meaningless. Stress arising from inadequate role authority is negatively related to job and management because of the fact that the employee finds himself to be insignificant and powerless. This develops a feeling of inferiority among the employees and the needs like self-expression and self–actualization remains unfulfilled. This situation contributes to job stress which affects their job performance.

Role Ambiguity

If the role is not clearly defined, person who is carrying out these activities will not behave as others expect him to when there is lot of uncertainties regarding job definition or expectation then people experience role ambiguity. Role ambiguity is particularly strong among managerial jobs were responsibilities are more general in nature and role definitions and task specifications are not clear, this causes stress.

Role Conflict

This occurs when the messages from the others about the

role are clear but contradictory or mutually exclusive. One common form is inter-role conflict between roles for example acting as subordinate to the boss and acting as spouse at home. Balancing are satisfying these roles is difficult and causes stress. Another form is intra-role conflict which may occur when the person gets conflicting demands from the different sources within the context of same role example pressure from the boss and pressure from the subordinate causes stress.

Working Conditions

The existence of poor working conditions can also cause stress to the employee. The environmental stressors could be extreme temperature, loud noise, too much or too little light, excess air pollution and so on. The effects of such environmental stressors are cumulative over a period of time and can have a negative effect on job performance. Another associated problem is with city and town extensions every common sight today people are forced to travel long distances in order to reach their place of work. This long distance commuting coupled with long hours of work can also prove to be stressful for the employees.

Interpersonal Relations

Work groups and work teams can also affect the behaviour and job performance of individual employees. Having good relationship with colleagues, subordinates and superiors not only ensures a better organizational behaviour but can also help employees to achieve both individual as well as organizational goals. Thus it is the interpersonal relationship which can influence the way in which employees may react to the various forms of job stress.

Effects of Stress

In short, the effects of stress can be broadly categorized into 3 areas.

Physiological Effects

These could take the form of increased blood pressure, increased heart rate, excessive sweating, frequent hot and cold spells, breathing problems, muscular problems so on.

Emotional Effects

These include anger, anxiety, nervousness, irritability, depression, low self-esteem, unhappiness with superior and job dissatisfaction.

Behavioural Effects

Work stress can cause individual behaviour changes visible in the form of absenteeism, higher turnover rates, frequent lapse in job performance, alcohol dependency and other drug abuses, improper communication and so on.

ROLE OF MANAGERS IN CREATING A CONSCIOUS ORGANIZATIONAL CULTURE TO REDUCE STRESS

The manager is the single greatest potential influence on the organizational culture. The manager can provide confidence and aware leadership and thus create a conscious culture of awareness and innovation, or can provide unconscious leadership and watch a series of sub-cultures be created around them, possibly without even being aware of them, or in fact can provide anti-conscious leadership and create culture of fear and blame.

The culture of organization that has a conscious manager is characterized by a focus on integrity, trust, creativity, intuition, freedom, flexibility and generosity. There is shift from control to trust, fear to truth, privilege to equality and fragmentation to unity. The conscious manager knows what culture he wants and establish the processes to ensure that culture is implemented.

The culture created by an anti-conscious manager is typically autocratic, uncaring, fear driven with attempts to control everything. There is a general underlying fear of invalidation and reprisals, and a distinct lack of sharing information. In this type of environment, staff will only provide information they know the manager is able to accept, and will go to great lengths to filter, manipulate or hide information they perceive will cause a reaction.

This is not a group effort, rather an understanding by the manager to create a conscious culture. The first and foremost the manager must recognize and acknowledge what culture is like now. While is it the way it is and how he had allowed it to be that way? What impact is it having on the organization? What is driving it to be that way? What is it going to take for it to change? Next, the manager need to be able to describe what kind of culture is required and how does this connect to the organization vision and strategy.

In understanding and developing conscious culture the manager has to—

- ➢ Understand the culture of the organization in a deeper sense. To understand deeply the manager must consider 3 key areas.
- ➢ Vision, values and strategy of the organization.

The manager has to understand the organization vision, values and strategy and ask himself what is the culture he wish to create that will drive the vision, values and strategy of the organization

- ➢ Accountability and transparency.

The manager has to ask himself

- What messages he must putout regarding accountability and transparency.
- What disclosures he should provide regarding processes, procedure and assumptions?

- ➢ Internal and external relationships.

The manager can ask himself

- What type of relations he wish to facilitate to the external parties?
- What type of internal relationships he wish to create about team work or treat the staffs as if they were his customers?

- ➢ Another tool to create conscious culture is that the manager must live in the question.

Conscious leader use question to encourage full participation and team work, to inspire creativity and encourage outside-the-box thinking, to empower others to solve problems resourcefully, etc. When the manager learnt to live in the question rather than being besieged by the problems or become vested in finding answers and solutions, he will be able to create his culture more consciously.

Managers through asking questions can cultivate a culture in which questions are welcomed, assumptions are investigated and new possibilities to solve problems are explored. Questions promote an inquisitive behaviour; build an innovative climate, a culture of accountability and a truly conscious organization.

- A manager must become a role model of what he would like the culture to be created.

This can be done by establishing mind set, behavior symbols and processes with regard to the way staff, stake holders and customers should be treated and the way business objectives should be pursued. The manager's behaviour and his decision must send a message to his staff of about how they are expected to behave, which in turn sets the cultural standard for others to follow.

- A conscious manager creates and articulates vision and strategy.

This provides the cohesion that enables all people to, at the very least, understand why they are doing what they do. Conscious leaders share this information freely and articulate the vision of the organization to those who have an interest in the organization.

- Conscious manager actively involve other and empower staff.

The manager must actively participate and involve other staff in decision-making which will create a culture of innovation. This will empower the staff and leads to creative expansion of the organization. This can be done by

- Willingness to receive all points of view by welcoming and hearing all perspectives, without resisting or reacting.
- Supporting staff to envision that there is no limit to what they could create by facilitating change constantly and encourage staff to discover more expansive and innovative ways of doing things

The culture of an organization powerfully shapes the identity and behavioural norms for the employees and stakeholders. It influences the employee's enthusiasm and impetus. The culture of an organization can be either expanding energy or sapping energy, depending on whether it is conscious, unconscious or anti-conscious. A truly conscious organization is where the manager chooses to embrace a culture of consciousness across the broad spectrum of the business concerns from strategic planning to recruit, to operating systems and processes; to developing the vision that guides the organization. The conscious manager creates a balanced integration of organizational vision, strategic and operational realities by encouraging and nurturing higher levels of conscious behaviour and attitude among the staff and stakeholders.

Thus, it is right to say that conscious managers create a stress free work force and develop a conscious culture for a healthy work environment.

Organizational Values and Behaviour

L. Anusha

Behind every human action there is ultimately a value. Personal values refer to a conception of what an individual or group regard as desirable.

- Values are a type of belief concerned with what is good or desirable.
- Values are enduring.
- Values motivate behaviour and guide evaluations and decisions.
- Value is very much a part of person's personality and a group's morale.

ORGANIZATIONAL VALUES

Business is one of the important functions of any modern society. For each business and profession, ultimately there are certain values which are adopted and honoured because without such coherence of values is not possible to have orderly, smooth and positive developments.

- A benign attitude to labour welfare is a value which may prompt an industrialist to do much more for workers than the labour laws stipulate.
- Service-mindedness is a value, which when cherished in an organization, manifests in better customer satisfaction.
- Within organization, values are imparted by founder entrepreneur or a dominant chief executive.
- The Organization's values must be in line with its purpose or mission, and the vision that it is trying to achieve.

RELATIONSHIP BETWEEN ORGANIZATION VALUES AND ORGANIZATIONAL BEHAVIOUR

Organizational values define the acceptable standards which govern the behaviour of individuals within an organization. Without such values, individuals will pursue behaviour that are in line with their own individual system, this may lead to behaviours that the organization does not wish to encourage. So to summarize, articulated values of an organization can provide a framework for collective leadership of an organization to encourage common norms of behaviour which will support the achievement of the organization's goal and missions.

LIVING VALUES—THE WAY TO ORGANIZATIONAL CULTURE

1. Communicate the values frequently
   - Thank those people who have achieved something which particularly emphasizes the values.
2. Make values explicitly available
   - As new members join an organization.

3. Revisit and refresh the values.
   - Allowing members to update them.
   - Refresh and reassess values regularly.
4. Confront contradictory behaviour
   - If contradictory values are practiced—communicate and confront.
   - More danger when dynamic, dominant individuals espouse the contradictory values.
5. Periodically check out with feedback.
   - Ask people what they think are the values of your organization.
   - The people are not just employees, but also others who may be influenced by the stated values.
   - Suppliers, customers, consultants and former employees.

ALIGNING ORGANIZATIONAL BEHAVIOUR TO ORGANIZATIONAL VALUES

"Clarify values to people rather than impose them"

Level 1 Create an awareness that people who have values of their own are more idealistic.

Level 2 Given a set of values ask people to choose some cherished values.

Level 3 Segregation of compatible values and incompatible values.

Level 4 Create a sense of satisfaction in scope for pursuing their values.

Level 5 Identify the process values that will lead towards practicing their values or realistic skills essential to practice it.

Level 6 Thus value clarification inputs to break the inner barriers that were obstructing the practice of values.

"Values combined with powerful vision can turbo-charge us to scale new heights and make us succeed beyond our wildest expectations".

"Values not only help in achieving success but also make success more enduring and lasting".

"Values can help establish business or career purpose".
—by Azim Premji, Chairman Wipro Corporation

There are five basic principles to be followed by all organization to power the behaviour with ethical values.

Five P's namely

Purpose	☞ Mission of organization guided by values.
Pride	☞ Proud of yourselves and your organization.
Patience	☞ Holding to ethical values lead to success in long-term.
Persistence	☞ Committed to commitment, actions consistent with purpose.
Perspective	☞ Time to pause and reflect, take stock: • Where you are? • Evaluate where you are going? • How you are going? • How to reach there?

Corporate Goals and Vision

M. Rajeswari

"Vision without action is a day dream. Action without vision is a nightmare".

—*Japanese proverb*

CORPORATE GOALS

The goals of an organization determine the nature of its inputs and outputs, the series of activities through which outputs are achieved and interactions with its external environment. The major outcome of strategic road-mapping and strategic planning, after gathering all necessary information, is the setting of goals for the organization based on its vision and mission statement. A goal is a long-range aim for a specific period. It must be specific and realistic. Long-range goals set through strategic planning are translated into activities that will ensure reaching the goal through operational planning.

CORPORATE VISION

"To achieve great things, you need ambitious visions. And it does not matter that vision cannot be laid out in details. It is the direction that counts".

Corporate vision is a short, succinct, and inspiring statement of what the organization intends to become and to achieve at some point in the future, often stated in competitive terms. Vision refers to the category of intentions that are broad, all-inclusive and forward thinking. It is the image that a business must have of its goals before it sets out to reach them. It describes aspirations for the future, without specifying the means that will be used to achieve those desired ends.

The corporate success depends on the vision articulated by the chief executive or the top management. For a vision to have any impact of the employees of an organization it has to be conveyed in a dramatic and enduring way. The most effective visions are those that inspire, usually asking employees for the best, the most or the greatest. Make sure you keep stretch in your vision, communicate it constantly, and keep linking the events of today to your vision, understanding the relationship between the two.

SETTING GOALS

The major outcome of strategic road-mapping and strategic planning, after gathering all necessary information, is the setting of goals for the organization based on its vision and mission statement. A goal is a long-range aim for a specific period. It must be specific and realistic. Long-range goals set through strategic planning are translated into activities that will ensure reaching the goal through operational planning.

When setting goals, keep these points in mind:

- They should be realistic and attainable.
- They should improve the organization (moral, monetary, etc.).
- Your people should be involved in the goal-setting process.

- A program should be developed to achieve each goal.

The goal of an organization determine the nature of its inputs and outputs, the series of activities through which outputs are achieved and interactions with its external environment.

There are four characteristics of goal-setting:

- *Goal difficulty*—Increasing you employee's goal difficulty increases their challenge and enhances the amount of effort expended to achieve them. The more difficult goals lead to increased performance if they seem feasible. If they seem too high, employees will give up when they fail to achieve them.
- *Goal specificity*—When given specific goals, employees tend to perform higher. Telling them to do their best or giving no guidance increases ambiguity about what is expected. Employees need a set goal or model in order to display the correct behaviour.
- *Feedback*—Providing feedback enhance the effects of goal setting. Performance feedback keeps their behaviour directed on the right target and encourages them to work harder to achieve the goal.
- *Participation in Goal-setting*—Employees who participate in the process, generally set higher goals than if the goals were set for them. It also affects their belief that the goals are obtainable and increases their motivation to achieve them.

MISSION STATEMENTS AND VISION STATEMENTS

Organizations sometimes summarize goals and objectives into a mission statement and/or a vision statement:

- *A Mission statement*: tells you what the company is now. It concentrates on present; it defines the customer(s), critical processes and it informs you about the desired level of performance.

- *A Vision statement*: outlines what a company wants to be. It concentrates on future; it is a source of inspiration; it provides clear decision-making criteria.

Feature of an effective vision statement may include:

- Clarity and lack of ambiguity
- Paint a vivid and clear picture, not ambiguous
- Describing a bright future (hope)
- Memorable and engaging expression
- Realistic aspirations, achievable
- Alignment with organizational values and culture, rational
- Time bound if it talks of achieving any goal or objectives

It is important here to distinguish between "vision" and "mission" for the organization. Vision is often referred to as "skyhooks for the soul". In fact, vision is that igniting spark that can inspire and energize people to do better. The focus of vision is to reach out hungrily for the future and drag it into the present. To quote Tom Peters, "developing a vision and living it vigorously are essential elements of leadership". The latest trend in many organizations is to apply the "VIP" approach, i.e. "Vision Integrated Performance."

To become really effective, an organizational vision statement must (the theory states) become assimilated into the organization's culture. Leaders have the responsibility of communicating the vision regularly, creating narratives that illustrate the vision, acting as role-models by embodying the vision, creating short-term objectives compatible with the vision, and encouraging others to craft their own personal vision compatible with the organization's overall vision.

FUNCTIONS OF GOALS

Goals

- Provide guidelines for decision-making and justification for actions taken.
- Influence the structure of the organization and help determine the nature of technology employed.

- Provide a standard of performance

INFORMAL AND FORMAL GOALS

Informal goals may be inferred from the actual decisions made and actions taken within the organization. Formal goals are officially stated.

PRIMARY OBJECTIVES

The primary objectives of an organization may be seen as:

- To continue to exist—survive,
- To maintain growth and development, and
- To make a profit.

CLASSIFICATION OF ORGANIZATIONAL GOALS

Etzioni classifies organizational goals in terms of their relationship with the concept of power and compliance:

- Order goals—negative and attempt to place some kind of restraint upon members,
- Economic goals—concerned with the production of goods/services to people outside the organization, and
- Culture goals—concerned with symbolic objects and with creating or maintaining the value systems of society.

A SYSTEM VIEW OF ORGANIZATIONAL GOALS

- *Consumer goals*: the nature of output in terms of markets served and consumer satisfaction,
- *Product goals*: the nature and characteristics of the outputs,
- *Operational goals*: the series of activities involved in providing outputs and the operation and functioning of the organization, and
- *Secondary goals*: those not related to the main aims of the organization.

A systems view of organizational goals and objectives

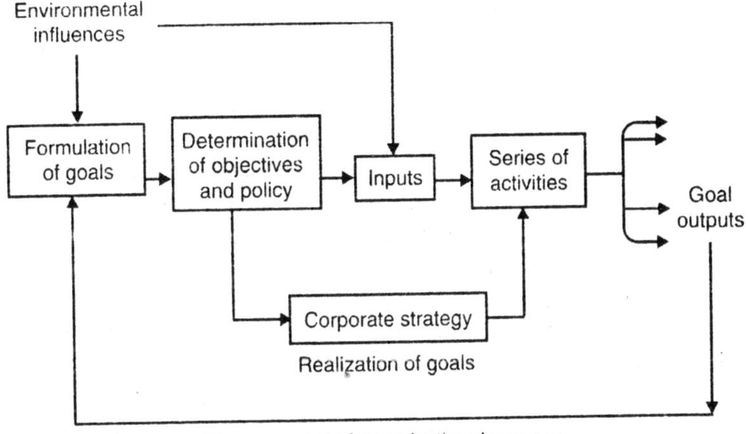

Example:

Queensland University of Technology

Vision and Goals

QUT is a leading university of technology which aims to strengthen its distinctive national and international reputation by combining academic strength and practical engagement with the world of the professions, industry, government and the broader community.

In line with this aim, QUT's overall vision for the future is:

- To provide outstanding learning environments and programs that lead to excellent outcomes for graduates, enabling them to work in and guide a world characterized by increasing change;
- To undertake high-impact research and development in selected areas, at the highest international standards, reinforcing the University's applied emphasis and securing significant commercials and practical outcomes; and
- To strengthen and extend the University's strategic

partnerships with professional and broader communities to reflect both its academic ambitions and its civic responsibility.

Five key goals will guide QUT's progress towards attaining this vision:

- To build research capacity in selected areas;
- To strengthen the University's reputation for quality teaching and learning and provide among the best learning environment in Australia;
- To strengthen the University's "real-world" positioning in teaching and research through better partnerships across internal and external boundaries;
- To integrate information and communication technology into teaching, research, business support functions and infrastructure; and
- To develop environments that foster and reward high-quality scholarship and that build a sense of community.

Good organizations convey a strong vision of where they will be in the future. As a leader, you have to get your people to trust you and be sold on your vision. Using the leadership tools described in this guide and being honest and fair in all you do will provide you with the ammo you need to gain their trust. To sell them on your vision, you need to possess energy and display a positive attitude that is contagious. People want a strong vision of where they are going. No one wants to be struck in a dead-end company going nowhere . . . or a company headed in the wrong direction. They want to be involved with a winner! And your people are the ones who will get you to that goal. You cannot do it alone!

Set a common goal. Mobilize your people around a common goal. Help them feel a part of something genuine, special and important and you'll inspire real passion and loyalty.

Organizational Vision and Culture

P.D. RAJESWARI

Both people and organizations need to establish a strategic framework for significant success. This framework consists of:

- A vision for the future,
- A mission that defines what the company does,
- Values that shape its actions,
- Strategies that zero in on guide its key success approaches,
- Goals and action plan to do the daily, weekly and monthly by each of these important concepts, a mission that defines what you are doing,
- Values that shape your actions,
- Strategies that zero in on key success approaches, and
- Goals and action plan to do the daily, weekly and monthly actions.

VISION, MISSION AND VALUES

Vision tells us where organization wants to be in the future. It reflects the optimistic view of the organization's future.

Mission tells us where the organization is going now, basically describing the purpose, why this organization exists.

Values protect the organization during the progression, reflecting the organization's culture and priorities.

Vision Statement

A vision is a statement about what your organization wants to become. It should be reasonable with all members of the organization and help them feel proud, excited and part of something much bigger than themselves. A vision should stretch the organization's capabilities and image of itself. It gives shape and direction to the organization's future. Visions range in length from a couple of words to several pages are recommended. Shorter vision statements are recommended, because people will tend to remember their shorter organizational vision.

Many people mistake vision statement for mission statement. The vision describes a future identity and the mission describes why it will be achieved. A mission statement defines the purpose of broader goal for being in existence or in the business. It serves as an ongoing guide without time frame. The mission can remain the same for decades if crafted well. Vision is more specific in terms of objective and future state. Vision is related to some form of achievement if successful.

A mission statement can resemble a vision statement in a few companies, but that can be a grave mistake. It can confuse people. The vision statement can galvanize the people to achieve defined objectives, even if they are stretch objectives, provided the vision is SMART (Specific, Measurable, Achievable, Relevant and Time bound). A mission statement provides a path to realize the vision in line with its values. These statements have a direct bearing on the bottom line and success of the organization.

Which comes first? The mission statement or the vision statement? For example, in an established business where the mission is established, then many times, the mission guides the vision where the company is, its current resources or current obstacles, and where it wants to go.

Core Values

Values are traits or qualities that are considered worthwhile; they represent an individual's highest priorities and deeply held driving forces. (Values are also known as core values and as governing values; they all refer to the same sentiment).

Value statements are grounded in values and define how people want to behave with each other in the organization. They are statements about how the organization will value customers, suppliers, and the internal community. Value statements describe actions which are the living enactment of the fundamental values held by most individuals within the organization.

The values of each of the individuals in your workplace, along with their experience, upbringing and so on, meld together to form you corporate culture. The values of your senior leaders are especially important in the development of your culture. These leaders have a lot of power in your organization to set the course and environment and they have selected the staff for your workplace.

Basically, organizational culture is the personality of the organization. Culture comprises of the assumptions, values, norms and tangible signs (artifacts) of organization members and their behaviours. Members of an organization soon come to sense the particular culture of an organization.

Organizational culture, or corporate culture, comprises the attitudes, experiences, beliefs and values of an organization. It has been defined as "the specific collection of values and norms that are shared by people and groups in an organization and that control the way they interact with each other and with stakeholders outside the organization. Organizational values are beliefs and ideas about what kinds of goals members of an organization should pursue and ideas about the appropriate kinds or standards of behaviour organizational members should use to achieve these goals. From organizational values develop organizational norms, guidelines or expectations that prescribe appropriate kinds of behaviour by employees in particular situations and control the behaviour of organizational members towards one another".

According to Campbell it is concerned with how employees perceive the six basic characteristics-individual, autonomy, structure, reward, consideration and conflict. Keith Davis points out certain values that affect work viz. freedom, equality, security and opportunity.

When one wants to change an aspect of the culture of an organization one has to keep in consideration that this is a long-term project. Corporate culture is something that is very hard to change and employees need time to get used to the new way of organizing. For companies with a very strong and specific culture it will be even harder to change.

Keith Davis points out certain values that affect work, that is freedom, equality, security and opportunity.

Cummings & Worley give the following six guidelines for cultural change; these changes are in line with the eight distinct states mentioned by Kotter:

1. *Formulate a clear strategic vision*: In order to make an effective cultural change a clear vision of the firm's new strategy, shared values and behaviours is needed. This vision provides the intention and direction for the culture change.
2. *Display top-management commitment*: It is very important to keep in mind that culture change must be managed from the top of the organization, as willingness to change of the senior management is an important indicator. The top of the organization should be very much in favour of the change in order to actually implement the change in the rest of the organization.
3. *Show the Management Team*: In order to show that the management team is in favour of the change, the change has to be notable at first at this level. The behaviour of the management needs to symbolize the kinds of values and bahaviours that should be realized in the rest of the company. It is important that the management shows the strengths of the current culture

as well, it must be made clear that the current organizational does not need radical changes, but just a few adjustments.

4. *Modify the organization to support organizational change*: The fourth step is to modify the organization to support organizational change.
5. *Select and socialize newcomers and terminate deviants*: A way to implement a culture is to connect it to organizational membership, people can be selected and terminated in terms of their fit with the new culture.
6. *Develop ethical and legal sensitivity*: Changes in culture can lead to tensions between organizational and individual interests, which can result in ethical and legal problems for practitioners.

Strong and Weak Culture

Strong culture is said to exist where staff respond to stimulus because of their alignment to organizational values.

Conversely, there is weak culture where there is little alignment with organizational values and control must be exercised through extensive procedures and bureaucracy.

Specific Cultural Values and Management Styles

S. Abdul Sajid

Culture according to a widely accepted definitions, is the integrated pattern of human knowledge, belief and behaviour. Culture thus defined consists of languages, ideas, beliefs, customs, taboos, codes, institutions tools techniques, work of art, rituals, ceremonies, and other related components and the development of culture depends upon men's capacity to learn and to transmit knowledge to succeeding generations.

Culture plays an important role in the lives of organizational members. Enmeshed in a set of shared values, norms and meanings, it helps to promote organizational objectives. It is a framework for understanding and attributing meaning to the structures, systems, events, instructions and other phenomena that take place in organizations. Every time people come together with a shared purpose, culture is created within a group. This group of people could be a family, neighbourhood, project team or company. Culture is automatically created out of the combined thoughts, energies and attitudes of the people in group.

Culture is an energy force that becomes woven through the thinking, behaviour, and identity of those within the group. Culture is powerful and invisible and its manifestations are far reaching. Culture determines a company's dress code, work environment, work hours, rules for getting ahead and getting promoted, how the business world is viewed, what is valued, who is valued and much more.

KEY COMPONENTS OF CULTURE

A common way of understanding culture sees it as consisting of four elements that are "passed on from generation to generation by learning alone":

1. Values; 2. Norms; 3. Institutions; 4. Artifacts.

Values comprise ideas about what in life seems important. They guide the rest of the culture. Norms consist of expectations of how people will behave in various situations. Each culture has methods called *sanctions*, of enforcing its norms. Sanctions vary with the importance of the norm; norms that a society enforces formally have the status of laws. Institutions are the structures of a society within which values and norms are transmitted. Artifacts—things or aspects of material culture—derive from a culture's values and norms.

Corporate culture is the specific collection of values and norms that are shared by people and groups in an organization and that control the way they interact with each other and with stakeholders outside the organization. Organizational values are beliefs and ideas about the appropriate kinds or standards of behaviour organization members should use to achieve these goals. From organizational values develop organizational norms; guidelines or expectations that prescribe appropriate kinds of behaviour by employees in particular situation and control the bahaviour of organizational members towards one another (Strategic management, Charles, W.L., Hill Gareth, R. Jones, fifth edition, 2001).

Every organization has an existing culture. For most, the good news is that their existing culture, while containing a few bad elements, is largely in good shape. The task, therefore, is not to create or invent a new culture, but to identify what exists, assess where improvements are needed, develop an action plan and implement it. Complex organizations may have a number of sub=cultures. The existence of sub-culture crates interesting challenges for corporations. As we identify more and more sub-cultures we gain the ability to improve effectiveness by fine tuning the delivery of our compliance and ethics programme.

Visible manifestations of culture:

- Dress code
- Work environment
- Benefits
- Perks
- Conversations
- Work/life balance
- Titles and job description
- Organizational structure

Invisible manifestations of culture:

- Values
- Private conversation
- Invisible rules
- Attitudes
- Beliefs
- Worldviews
- Moods and emotions
- Unconscious interpretations
- Standards of bahaviour
- Paradigms
- Assumptions

Establishment of Values

The values are made up of everything that has happened to anybody in their life and include influences from their parents and family, their religious affiliations, their friends and peers, their education, their reading, and more. Effective people recognize these environmental influences and identify and develop a clear, concise, and meaningful set of values/beliefs, and priorities. Once defined, values impact every respect of their life.

Values are traits or qualities that are considered worthwhile; they represent the highest priorities and deeply held driving forces. An individual is a part of any organization, he brings the deeply held values and beliefs to the organization. There they co-mingle with those of the other members to create an organization or family culture.

Importance of Personal Values

Personal values are a basic statement of what is most important to us as human being. Honesty, Shuracracy, Masawath, Sabr, Falah, Hikmath, and Fayyazi are some of the values that make up the core of our beliefs about ourselves and how want other people to perceive us.

It is also important to note that in any relationship, either inside or outside of the work environment, we tend to judge other people on the basis of our own values—not theirs. Without a clear context being set at the outset, and actively reinforced by executives and their top leadership team, conflict can occur when people feel that their own unique personal values are being transgressed. Ultimately, this can result in what is known as 'personal withdrawal'.

VALUES AND MANAGEMENT STYLES

Leaders or managers succeed or fail in inspiring peak performance, not only according to their ability to appreciate the values and motives of those whom they direct, but also according to their willingness to align their own managerial styles to the personal, situational and organizational environment. The bottom line of every effective leader is to deliver the results. Since management is also an art, every leader or manager has a personalized way of doing things.

This personalized manner manifests itself in the various managerial styles that are employed by different managers. Every management style has its own strengths and weaknesses, which exhibit different levels of effectiveness in different work situations. Management style is a function of one's own motives and values as well as what one has learned and experienced in life.

Leaders have to understand what motive their followers, their strength and weaknesses, and how they can function under stress. Most importantly, managers can discover how to build good working relationships by modifying their personal traits. Relationships are the heart of any business or organization. Productivity depends on the quality of relationships between departments, managers, co-workers and subordinates.

Influence of Islamic Values on Management Style

Islamic ontology presents a dual worldview: he mundane world and the life hereafter. What man does (in all area) in his short life affects his prospects in the life hereafter. Islam bestows a high degree of responsibility on man. All magnificent Allah created man in his own image and to be his khalifa (vicegerent) to carry out his divine will on earth. Thus, 'khalifa' implies trust and responsibility, authority and duty, election and service. Man holds a high position in the hierarchy of all known creatures due to his rational faculties and spiritual aspirations. However, this commendable supremacy is not a bed of roses as it engenders responsibility. As God's trustworthy agent, he is necessarily imbued with authority and power but in addition honour and integrity. His position confers upon him certain rights over other fellow creatures.

The teachings of Islam and qualities of human beings lead the executives towards the democratic orientation. There are several components that help people much towards democratic orientation. Some of them are : (a) love orientation (b) freedom orientation (c) love of life, and (d) Akhirath. These values are instrumental for democratic orientation.

(a) *Love Orientation*: These Islamic values will develop the love orientation among the executives. Shuracracy, Masawath, Adalah, Sabr, Sacrifice, Fayyazi, Trust, Tolerances, Humbleness, Forgiveness, Truthfulness, etc.

(b) *Freedom Orientation*: These values develop the freedom orientation—Tawhid, Risalath, Akirath, Falah (Salvation).

(c) *Biofilia Orientation*: These values develop the biofilia (love of life) orientation—Amanah, Muhasaba, Contentment, Thankfulness, Generosity, Adalah, Halal and Haram.

(d) *Akhirath Orientation*: These values develop Akhirath orientation—Taqdeer (fate), Ehsan, Accountability, etc.

Influence of Western Values of Leadership Style

The autocrat in the executive shows up his face when his attitude towards others is not properly groomed. Autocrat managers are usually perceived as ones who put the immediate task above all other considerations. They are less effective in that they make it obvious that they have no concern for relationship and have little confidence in other people. While many fear them, they also dislike them and are thus motivated to work well only when under direct pressure. Autocratic managers cannot understand why so many people are non-cooperative.

Autocratic managers are perceived as ones who believe that the average human being prefers to be directed, wishes to avoid responsibility, has relatively little ambition and wants security above all. Autocrat managers thus do not fully utilize the capabilities of others.

Corporate culture refers to the shared values, attitudes, standards and beliefs that characterize members of an organization. In a healthy corporate culture, employees view themselves as part of team and gain satisfaction from helping the overall company success. When employees feel that they are contributing to a successful group effort, their level of commitment and productivity, and thus the quality of the company's products or services are likely to improve. It is essential to develop the Islamic culture in the organization. This is a root for developing the democratic management style among the leaders.

Employee Retention Strategy

V. Shenbagapriya

The culture of an organization always goes a long way in deciding how the employees contribute. The companies usually fail to focus on how they can build the right kind of internal work culture, passion, pride, in the organization is what induces employees to stay back. Therefore, retention is core to grooming of a healthy body of employees.

Those who value and recognize their employees and understand their needs and aspiration will direct the future of the organization. For building a quality workforce, each organization must understand what motivates their employees to perform well and reward and reinforce those very things in order to get the best out of them.

REASONS FOR LEAVING A JOB

In most organizations different departments of HR with little or no coordination between them look after hiring and retention efforts.

Understand that hiring practices and retention polices go hand in hand and can result in formulating and implementing better people management strategies.

The 4 M's—Money, Mentoring, Matching expectations and Maintenance, hint if a person is likely to leave that job early.

MONEY

Money is an important offer component, which greatly influences a person's decision to join a firm. However, if hiring mangers focus exclusively on money to lure potential candidates it can result in future retention problems. A person who has accepted a job solely on monetary considerations is more likely to quit when a bigger offer comes his way. Yet, some hiring managers try to hire people as cheaply as possible. This might result in a short-term gain for the company but in the long-run, there can be a breakdown of loyalty. A person who accepts a low salary offer will do so only as a stop gap arrangement and quit when he gets a good offer elsewhere.

Solutions to money-related retention problems would be to keep salaries close to the industry average and focus on job branding. Offering a challenging work environment, scope for creativity, training opportunities, faster growth rate and better work life balance help attract people who look beyond money while accepting an offer.

MENTORING

Strong mentoring support from peers and superiors instills loyalty among new recruits. It is always better to recruit candidates from employee referrals than other sources. This is because those making a referral have a personal interest in the success of individuals referred. They offer guidance to the new recruits and help them adjust well to the organizational culture. An analysis of turnover rates from each source of recruits can throw light on factors contributing to the turnover. A well conceived on boarding and orientation programme that helps new employees to build good interpersonal relationships within the organization can greatly contribute towards reducing attrition rates due to lack of proper mentoring and guidance.

MATCHING EXPECTATIONS

New hires become frustrated when their initial expectations are not met. When the tall promises made at the time of hiring about work, technology or environment does not get reflected in the actual job, the new recruits are likely to get disillusioned. This is a potential factor that can contribute to early departure of the new hires. The hiring managers must not think that their responsibility ends once the recruitment process is complete. They should coordinate with other HR departments to see that the new recruits do not suffer on account of pad initial placement. They should advice reporting managers on ways to assign roles that match the expectations of new reports.

MAINTENANCE

Human resources are an important asset to any organization and they require a personalized maintenance schedule just like any other asset.

Performance appraisals, rewards, awards incentives and pay hikes are directed at maintaining the employees morale. But the department that focuses on the retention efforts will succeed in its endeavours provided it works closely with the hiring department and tailors its employee benefit programmes to suit the specific needs of employees. Gathering information on the average tenure of employees at their previous employers from the hiring department can help in estimating their likely tenure in the present job.

Before the employees start looking for new job, the organization can bring necessary changes in their job roles, titles and perks to keep their engagement levels intact. Attrition levels can be lowered to a large extent if the recruitment and retention functions are integrated.

RETAINING TALENT CHALLENGES TO HRM

The manager is not only to fill the demand for emerging job openings but also to retain the existing workforce. HR managers have to give up to retain their workforce a face the consequences of loosing their valuable manpower.

Executive Movements are not just at any specific tier of management. Right from the management trainers to senior level management, executive movements are prevalent. Gone are the days when people used to stick to one organization for their entire lifetime. Today being in an organization for more than a year means either the person is not really ambitious or something else is wrong.

WHY IS THIS HAPPENING?

(a) Changing Life Styles

Life styles have changed considerably since the past. People prefer to break away from the monotony of doing the same job over and over again. Now its about new jobs every coming year, new responsibilities and new work environment. People today think fast, act fast, and thus change their job faster.

(b) Death of Motivation

Full absence of motivation is cause for changing. Today's world whatever gives the best deal takes away the best talent. No matter what the job context or job content is, offer the best deal and corporate headquarters will be buzzing with the best brains in the industry.

(c) Increased Expectation

Employee expectation has increased recently. Whether the desire is reasonable or not, the employee may join for better salary given by new organizations.

(d) Increasing Opportunities

Another reason for changing is the rise in opportunities. While earlier job opportunities exist in non-traditional business.

(e) Assignments Abroad

People today are looking for international exposure, and any such exposure will help them expand their network and vision besides having a pay package in terms of dollars.

(f) Decreasing Loyalty Towards Organizations

Employee loyalty towards the organization has decreased considerably. Employees today are only loyal to their career and future prospects and loyalty towards organizations is hardly existent.

(g) Job Misfit

Sometimes in an effort to fill the gap, people are recruited fast without taking into consideration the job and competency fit. It only results in loss of man-hours and repetition of the whole process. So to avoid job misfit the selection of candidates, clarity of role and career objective is also considered. Sometime employee may join the company to get brand name only.

While salaries, peelers, challenges, designations and foreign assignment may derive people for sometime, most of the people also seek stability for themselves. Therefore, an HR manager needs to identify and create systems and processes that will retain employees.

WINNING EMPLOYEE COMMITMENT

Retention has become a significant HR and business imperative. HR executives are implementing various strategies to create a truly engaging environment where employees feel satisfied and connected with the organizations goals and objectives. Retention strategy is to bind the employee to the organization. The aim is to increase the commitment of an employee.

COMMITMENT

Commitment in the workplace can take various forms and arguably have the potential to influence organizational effectiveness and employee well-being. It is a force that binds an individual to a course of action of relevance to one or more targets. Commitment is a psychological state that binds the individual to the organization. It refers to the likelihood that an individual will stick to the organization, and feel psychologically attached to it, whether the job is satisfying or not.

Companies often mistake employee retention for commitment. It would be wrong to say that an employee who stays with the company is committed. An employee would stick to an organization because he may not have a better alternative or could be expecting similar work scenario at other places of employment and therefore, prefers to remain with the organization.

WINNING COMMITMENT

If firms want to win the true commitment of an employee, efforts needs to be initiated to enhance effective commitment.

(1) Organization Commitment Norm

Increasing with people who have served the organization for such a long tenure wends a signal that commitment is valued and respected in the organization.

(2) Organizational Dependability and Support

Gestures like these ensure that the affective and normative commitment of the employees increases and they become more committed towards the company.

(3) Advancement Opportunities

Growth is the essence of life. Organizations want growth and so do the people working for the organization. Of the major reasons for job hopping and seeking alternative employment opportunities is the lack of advancement opportunities within the organization. Sharing information related to growth opportunities will reduce continuance commitment and withdrawal cognition, reducing the overall attrition and turnover.

(4) Transparent Communication

Firms cannot expect their employees to be fully committed to the organization unless they ensure that the employees are integrated with the organizational soul. Employees will exhibit commitment of they start identifying with the value structure of the organization. This mutual trust cannot develop unless there is a transparent communication.

(5) Self-expression Opportunity

In today's knowledge economy, employees want to express their ideas and desire that the company provide adequate resources for them co-experiment. Research indicates that the companies that provide self-expression opportunities can win the commitment of their employees.

(6) Fostering Mentorship

It is an established fact that warm and healthy employee-supervisor relationship plays a significant role in building fondness and attachment for the workplace.

(7) Empowerment

The empowerment gives opportunity and platform to grow to the employees beyond their defined limits ensuring commitment. Empowerment is key to unlocking energy and encourages creativity and risk taking.

(8) Respecting Meritocracy

It is essential for firms to create an environment where employees are able to see the fairness of performance-based rewards. Meritocracy is a system by which advancements, appointments and promotions are based on performance and exceptional competency, rather than tenure or political favouritism.

Organizational culture is a set of characteristics that are commonly shared by people in the organization. The ultimate sources of organization culture is the people who makes up the organization. It is very important to be in touch with employees and interact with them constantly and consistently. It has been noticed that the higher the involvement, the greater will be the benefit for the organization. The strategies are required to put the "Right people in the right job" develop their skill set, reward the top performers retain key talents and increase efficiency of its workforce.

PART III

Organizational Dynamics : A Micro View

Future Ideal Corporate Culture

R. Subashini, N. Shivapriya and M. Venkata Chaithanya

CULTURE REFLECTS THE REALITIES OF PEOPLE WORKING TOGETHER EVERYDAY

Organizational Culture or corporate culture comprises the attitudes, experiences, beliefs and values of an organization. It has been defined as "the specific collection of values and norms that are shared by people and groups in an organization and that control the way they interact with each other and with stakeholders outside the organization". For example, an Entrepreneurial Organizational Culture (EOC) is a system of shared values, beliefs and norms of members of an organization, including valuing creativity and tolerance of creative people, believing that innovating and seizing market opportunities are appropriate behaviours to deal with problems of survival and prosperity, environmental uncertainty, and competitors' threats, and expecting organizational members to behave accordingly.

Organizational Values are beliefs and ideas about what kinds of goals members of an organization should pursue and ideas about the appropriate kinds or standards of behaviour organizational members should use to achieve these goals. From organizational values develop organizational norms, guidelines or expectations that prescribe appropriate kinds of behaviour by employees in particular situations and control the behaviour of organizational members towards one another.

Organizational Vision is a statement about what the organization wants to become. The vision should resonate with all members of the organization and help them feel proud, excited, and part of something much bigger than themselves. A vision should stretch the organization's capabilities and image of itself. It gives shape and direction to the organization's future.

For the past 25 years, the concept of Corporate Culture has gained wide acceptance as a way to understand human systems. From an "open-systems" perspective, each aspect of organizational culture can be seen as an important environmental condition affecting the system and its sub-systems. The examination of organizational culture is also a valuable analytical tool in its own right.

Edgar Schein, MIT Sloan School of Management professor, defines Corporate Culture as "the residue of success" within an organization. According to Schein, culture is the most difficult organizational attribute to change, outlasting organizational products, services, founders and leadership and all other physical attributes of the organization.

STRONG/WEAK CULTURE

Strong culture is said to exist where staff respond to stimulus because of their alignment to organizational values. Conversely, there is weak culture where there is little alignment with organizational values and control must be exercised through extensive procedures and bureaucracy. Where culture is strong—people do things because they believe it is the right thing to do—there is a risk of another phenomenon, Groupthink. "Groupthink" was described by Irving L. Janis as ". . . a quick and easy way to refer to a mode of thinking that people engage when they are deeply involved in a cohesive group, when members striving for unanimity override their motivation to realistically appraise alternatives of action."

This is a state where people, even if they have different ideas, do not challenge organizational thinking, and therefore there is a reduced capacity for innovative thoughts. This could occur, for example, where there is heavy reliance on a central charismatic figure in the organization, or where there is an evangelical belief in the organization's values, or also in groups where a friendly climate is at the base of their identity (avoidance of conflict). In fact groupthink is very common, it happens all the time, in almost every group. Innovative organizations need individuals who are prepared to challenge the *status quo*—be it groupthink or bureaucracy, and also need procedures to implement new ideas effectively.

Several studies have been made to classify organizational culture. To mention a few, Geert Hofstede demonstrated that there are national and regional cultural groupings that affect the behaviour of organizations. He identified five dimensions of culture in his study of national influences:

- *Power Distance*—The degree to which a society expects there to be differences in the levels of power. A high score suggests that there is an expectation that some individuals wield larger amounts of power than others. A low score reflects the view that all people should have equal rights.
- *Uncertainty Avoidance*—Reflects the extent to which a society accepts uncertainty and risk.
- *Individualism vs. Collectivism*—Individualism is contrasted with collectivism, and refers to the extent to which people are expected to stand up for themselves, or alternatively act predominantly as a member of the group or organization. However, recent researches have shown that high individualism may not necessarily mean low collectivism, and *vice versa*. Research indicates that the two concepts are actually unrelated. Some people and cultures might have both high individualism and high collectivism, for example. Someone who highly values duty to his or her group does not necessarily give a low priority to personal freedom and self-sufficiency.

- *Masculinity vs. Femininity*—Refers to the value placed on traditionally male or female values. Male values for example include competitiveness, assertiveness, ambition, and the accumulation of wealth and material possessions.
- *Long vs. Short-term orientation*—Describes a society's "time horizon," or the importance attached to the future *versus* the past and present. In long-term-oriented societies, thrift and perseverance are valued more; in short-term-oriented societies, respect for tradition and reciprocation of gifts and favours are valued more. (Eastern nations tend to score especially high here, with Western nations scoring low and the less developed nations very low; China scored highest and Pakistan lowest).

Deal and Kennedy defined organizational culture as *the way things get done around here*. They were able to suggest four classifications of organizational culture:

- *The Tough-Guy Macho Culture*: Feedback is quick and the rewards are high. This often applies to fast moving financial activities such as brokerage, but could also apply to a police force, or athletes competing in team sports. This can be a very stressful culture in which to operate.
- *The Work Hard/Play Hard Culture*: It's characterized by few risks being taken, all with rapid feedback. This is typical in large organizations, which strive for high quality customer service. It is often characterized by team meetings, jargon and buzzwords.
- *The Bet your Company Culture*: Here big stakes decisions are taken, but it may be years before the results are known. Typically, these might involve development or exploration projects, which take years to come to fruition, such as oil prospecting or military aviation.
- *The Process Culture*: It occurs in organizations where there is little or no feedback. People become bogged down with how things are done not with what is to be achieved. This is often associated with bureaucracies.

While it is easy to criticize these cultures for being overly cautious or bogged down in red tape, they do produce consistent results, which are ideal in, for example, public services.

ORGANIZATIONAL CULTURE AND CHANGE

When one wants to change an aspect of the culture of an organization one has to keep in consideration that this is a long-term project. Corporate culture is something that is very hard to change and employees need time to get used to the new way of organizing. For companies with a very strong and specific culture it will be even harder to change.

Cummings & Worley gave the following six guidelines for cultural change.

1. *Formulate a clear strategic vision*: In order to make a cultural change effective a clear vision of the firm's new strategy, shared values and behaviours is needed. This vision provides the intention and direction for the culture change.
2. *Display Top-management commitment*: It is very important to keep in mind that culture change must be managed from the top of the organization, as willingness to change of the senior management is an important indicator.
3. *Model culture change at the highest level*: It is important that the management shows the strengths of the current culture as well; it must be made clear that the current organizational does not need radical changes, but just a few adjustments.
4. *Modify the organization to support organizational change*: The fourth step is to modify the organization to support organizational change.
5. *Select and socialize newcomers and terminate deviants*: A way to implement a culture is to connect it to organizational membership, people can be selected and terminate in terms of their fit with the new culture.
6. *Develop ethical and legal sensitivity*: Changes in culture can lead to tensions between organizational and

individual interests, which can result in ethical and legal problems for practitioners. This is particularly relevant for changes in employee integrity, control, equitable treatment and job security.

LEADERSDHIP ENRICHED CULTURE

To survive and succeed in exercising leadership, leaders must also work as closely with opponents as they do with supporters. In fact, opponents deserve more of attention not only as a tactic of strategy and survival but also sometimes as a matter of compassion. The leader needs to create a holding environment. The leadership pattern has a great influence on the organizational culture. It is the leader who frames the organizational culture. He should include the following elements to enhance the organizations reputation in the global arena.

- *The Paradigm*: What the organization is about; what it does; its mission; its values.
- *Control Systems*: The processes in place to monitor what is going on. Role cultures would have vast rulebooks. There would be more reliance on individualism in a power culture.
- *Organizational Structures*: Reporting lines, hierarchies, and the way that work flows through the business.
- *Power Structures*: Who makes the decisions, how widely spread is power, and on what is power based?
- *Rituals and Routines*: Management meetings, board reports and so on may become more habitual than necessary.
- *Stories and Events*: Convey a message about what is valued within the organization

Under Leadership Enriched Culture, the leader's vital elements should be: (i) Commitment and (ii) Clarity of goals, both with respect to the task at hand. The extent of effectiveness depends upon the extent of these two factors—Commitment being the more dominant factor between the two. The leader who is high on commitment and clarity could change from one style of leadership to another and anywhere in that continuum, depending upon the need of the task/mission and the goals and sub-goals she/he has to achieve. The effective leader is effective because he is committed to the task and is clear about how to achieve it. The same leader may not be effective in another task that does not generate Commitment and Clarity in him. Thus, leadership is task-based, having a relationship with the factors of Commitment and Clarity of goals. Companies such as Tata's, Infosys are wonderful examples for a dynamic organizational culture. They have always set a standard for the other organizations. However, even after the introduction of new technologies and the growth of competitors these organizations have always stood at the forefront for the benefit of their customers.

I. THE TATA'S SPEAK—*Integrity-based Leadership*

The Tata Group is a multinational conglomerate based in Mumbai, India. In terms of market capitalization and revenues, Tata Group is the largest private company in India. It has interests in steel, automobiles, information technology, communication, power, tea and hotels. The Tata Group has operations in more than 85 countries across six continents and its companies export products and services to 80 nations.

The Tata Group comprises 98 companies in seven business sectors. Companies which form a major part of the group include Tata Steel, Corus Steel, Tata Motors, Tata Consultancy Services, Tata Tea, Tata Power, Tata Communications and the Taj Hotels. The group takes the name of its founder, Jamsedji Tata, a member of whose family has almost invariably been the chairman of the group. The current chairman of the Tata group is Ratan Tata, who took over from J.R.D. Tata in 1991. The company is currently in its fifth generation of family stewardship.

II THE INFOSYS SPEAK—*Value-based Leadership*

Founded in 1981 in Bangalore by Narayana Murthy and six colleagues, Infosys is consistently ranked as one of India's most respected firms across all industries, Infosys was a pioneer in strategic offshore outsourcing of software services.

Customer delight, Leadership by example, Integrity and transparency, Fairness and pursuit of Excellence are their parameters for Success. Younger employees are viewed as "the eyes and the ears of the company", bringing to the forefront contemporary issues that might otherwise be overlooked.

According to Mr. Narayana Murthy:

> "A leader is an agent of change, and progress is about change. In the words of Robert F. Kennedy, 'Progress is a nice word; but change is its motivator."

Leadership is about raising the aspirations of followers and enthusing people with a desire to reach for the stars. For instance, Mahatma Gandhi created a vision for independence in India and raised the aspirations of our people. Leadership is about making people say, 'I will walk on water for you.' It is about creating a worthy dream and helping people achieve it.

Adversity

A leader has to raise the confidence of followers. He should make them understand that tough times are part of life and that they will come out better at the end of it. He has to sustain their hope, and their energy levels to handle the difficult days. There is no better example of this than Winston Churchill. His courageous leadership as prime minister for Great Britain successfully led the British people from the brink of defeat during World War II. He raised his people's hopes with the words, 'These are not dark days; these are great days—the greatest days our country has ever lived.'

Values

The leader has to create hope. He has to create a plausible story about a better future for the organization: everyone should be able to see the rainbow and catch a part of it. This requires creating trust in people. And to create trust, the leader has to subscribe to a value system: a protocol for behaviour that enhances the confidence, commitment and enthusiasm of the people.

Governance

Good corporate governance is about maximizing shareholder value on a sustainable basis while ensuring fairness to all stakeholders: customers, vendor-partners, investors, employees, government and society. Successful organization tides over many downturns. The best index of success is its longevity. This is predicated on adhering to the finest levels of corporate governance.

At Infosys, we have consistently adopted transparency and disclosure standards even before law mandated it. In 1995, Infosys suffered losses in the secondary market. Under Indian GAAP (generally accepted accounting principles), we were not required to make this information public. Nevertheless, we published this information in our annual report.

Integrity

Strong leadership in adverse times helps win the trust of the stakeholders, making it more likely that they will stand by you in your hour of need. As leaders who dream of growth and progress, integrity is the most wanted attribute. Lead the teams to fight for the truth and never compromise on your values. I am confident that our corporate leaders, through honest and desirable behaviour, will reap long-term benefits for their stakeholders.

EXPERIENCES IN A NUTSHELL—POSITIVES AND NEGATIVES

"Experience is not what happens to a man. It is what a man does with what happens to him."

Ranbaxy Laboratories Ltd. (RLL) is the largest pharmaceutical company incorporated in India. It is also amongst the top league globally and is ranked 9th largest generic company worldwide. Ranbaxy is also credited with the tag of true Indian multinational. It is one of the first Indian pharmaceutical companies to start a joint venture abroad. Rapid growth of Ranbaxy is attributed mainly to its focused research, joint ventures in India and abroad. The success of Ranbaxy is due to the Innovative, Strategic Leadership style followed says chief executive Malvinder Singh.

RIL is the first and only private sector Company from India to feature in the Fortune Global 500 list of 'World's Largest Corporations' since 2004 and ranks amongst the world's Top 200 companies in terms of profits. RIL has been amongst the list of 25 fastest climbers ranked by Fortune. RIL emerged in the world's 10 most respected energy/chemicals companies and amongst the top 50 companies that create the most value for their shareholders in a global survey and research conducted by PricewaterhouseCoopers and Financial Times. The laurels of RIL is due to the Innovative Leadership Culture adapted by Shri Mukesh Ambani, Chairman and Managing Director, Reliance Industries Limited (RIL).

Ideal Corporate Culture is the description of what an organization does and describes the business the organization is in. It clearly gives the reason for the current existence of the organization. For any organization to excel—an ideal corporate culture is the need of the hour.

Strong winds of change are sweeping over the world of business. There are two basic currents—one of technology and another of globalization, each reinforcing the other. Technology has made globalization possible and globalization has made the growth and propagation of technology easier. The result has been an unprecedented connectivity between organizations and between people. The transport and movement of materials and people is quicker. The communication by voice transmission is almost instantaneous. The availability of such services is phenomenal, resulting in increased uniformity of cultures, similarity of role models and more openness of markets.

For such a rapidly changing environment Leadership Enriched Culture is pivotal. Leadership Enriched Culture is proposed with two vital elements in the making of effectiveness of leadership say, (i) Commitment, and (ii) Clarity of goals.

The extent of effectiveness depends upon the extent of these two factors—Commitment being the more dominant factor between the two. The leader who is high on commitment and clarity is task-based.

In conclusion, lets keep in mind two Sanskrit sentences: *Sathyannasti Paro Dharma* (there is no *dharma* greater than adherence to truth); and *Satyameva jayate* (truth alone triumphs). Let these be the motto for a perfect Leadership Enriching Culture.

Organizational Culture—Its Present Scenario in BPO's

G. Tamil Selvi

In many organizations, "culture" is often viewed merely as an intangible atmospheric condition that somehow contributes to performance. This is wrong; culture has to be shaped to enable achievement of goals.

Although structure and people systems influence an organization, culture which is more ethereal or soft plays a crucial role in the success of a company.

ORGANIZATIONAL CULTURE IN BPO's

BPO INDUSTRY—Some Statistics

- Over 2,50,000 people are employed in BPO sector and is expected to reach 1.1 million by 2008.
- Revenue of the sector touches $ 3.6 billion.
- Burn out stress syndrome is common among BPO employees.

- BPO industry lacks a regulatory framework from FDI.

NATURE OF WORK AT BPO's

The work condition in BPO's and call centres are different from conventional industrial mould. For the first time since they evolved BPO's are trying to shed their image as a fun place for youngsters to work.

To retain employees some BPO's went overboard with the fun theme. They even hired "Fun officers" who were paid to organize parties more often. But as the nature of work became complicated and the quality of work being outsourced become better, CEO's realized that the time to change work place culture had arrived.

PRESENT WORK CULTURE AT BPO's

- The "Fun and party" concept was promoted to get the work force but now even the quality of work force employed has changed.
- There is a line drawn between work and fun. The organization culture has been defined in terms of work place etiquettes.
- The BPO Co's have observed a change in the expectation of the candidates. Earlier the candidates were interested in the money, but now they look for career growth.

This is done in various companies within the industry in many ways:

- In-house career counsellors.
- Cross training—for inter-departmental function.
- MBA classes—Co's have tied up with IIM, NMIMS, XLRI, etc. where they bear 90% cost of courses.
- Technical Institute—Tie up with premier Technical Institute like IIT where employees can enroll for extra education.
- IJP—Internal job postings—Here a person from a different job role or function is trained and groomed

for a responsibility belonging to a totally different genus. This is a common practice in BPO's.

- Mentoring: It is one of the ways in which Co's mould future leaders.
- The dynamic and vibrant work environment acts as a great booster of employee morale, a stress buster and causes a change in the monotonous work schedule.
- Realizing the value of fun at work place, the HR professionals are taking special measures to incorporate the same in the Organizational Culture. Work and play Organization Culture plays an important role is the retention process of employees. HR initiatives for employee benefits by majority of BPO's:
- Group medi-claim insurance scheme.
- Personal accident insurance scheme.
- Subsidized food and transportation.
- Company leased accommodation.
- Recreation, cafeteria, ATM and concierge facilities.
- Corporate credit card.
- Cellular phone and Laptops.
- Personal Health Care programmes.
- Loan facilities.
- Educational benefits.
- Performance based incentives (which can be 22% of salary).
- Flexi time.
- Flexible salary benefits.
- Regular get together and other cultural programs.
- Wedding day gift.
- Employee referral scheme.
- Employee stock option plan.
- Work place politics also affects organizational culture besides causing problems for the individual who work together, employees and managers concentrate on the political aspect of work and may have less time to pay attention to their jobs. This translates into financial loss, which may inturn translate into job loss.

The new work places are characterized by flat and non-bureaucratic organizational structure, informal relationships emphasis on team-work and flexible management policies. They offer non-hierarchical work culture, employee friendly human resources policies, attractive working environments and high salaries. But at the same time the industry is known for its high-pressure work atmosphere and long working hours which create high level of stress, employee dissatisfaction and high attrition rates.

Some ways to learn new culture:

- Interview interaction
- Online information
- Networking with friends
- Transition phrase
- Team dynamics

Better interaction help avoid culture shock on the surface.

To Conclude

The culture of an organization and HR practices are more important as predictors of business performance.

If organizations are going to get the discretionary behaviours from individuals who are so important to business performance, they must work to create supportive cultures which encourage innovation and performance.

Any successful business needs a strong and positive culture to act as the engine to drive performance and yet still, few businesses fully understand the relationships between the input of culture and the output of results.

Building Organizational Culture that Stimulates Creativity

S. KAMALAKKANNAN

Organization culture is the integral pattern of human behaviour that includes thoughts, speech and action and depends on man's capacity for learning and transmitting knowledge to succeeding generation. Most elements of a culture take a long time in their evolution and equally as long to change. An organization has a mission when its culture fits with strategy. The determinants are strategy, structure, support mechanism, that encourages innovation and open communication values, norms and beliefs that play a role in creativity.

Business forms also have their distinctive cultures. It is sum total of the norms, beliefs and values that regulate the behaviour of individuals and groups within any given corporation many forms are not even aware of their culture or sensitive to its distinct characteristics.

To strengthen an organization culture, a set of values, behaviour characteristics and role models for the professionals working in an organization should be identified. Structure reflects the organization of work into roles. The roles may be in production, finance, marketing, personnel, etc.,

Cultural Analysis

There are five primary cultural elements that are examined during cultural analysis.

Elements of Culture

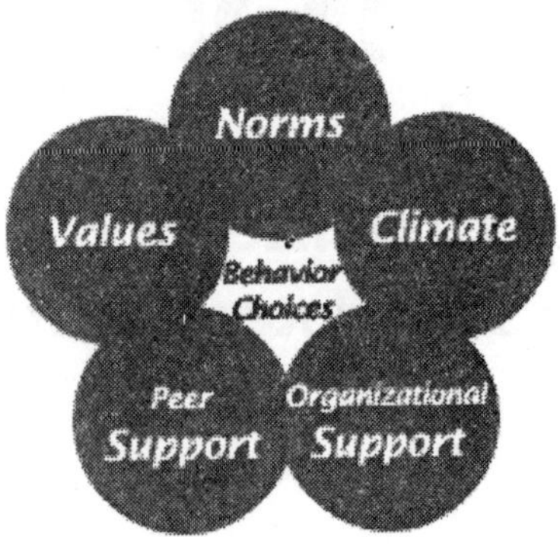

Values

Values are heartfelt beliefs about the appropriate way to behave. Values constitute the should and shouldn't of individual and cultural life. While the concept is most familiar on an individual level, groups, organizations and communities also adopt values.

Norms

A norm is an expected and accepted behaviour: "It's the way we do things around here." These social standards of behaviour may or may not be consistent with individual or cultural values.

Climate

Some cultures embrace needed change while other cultures are highly resistant. Three attributes seem to determine a culture's receptivity to change—sense of community, shared vision and positive outlook.

A sense of community is present when people feel as if they belong and trust one another. This sense of belonging includes an awareness that others "care" and that the individual, in turn, has a responsibility to care for others. With a sense of community people are not viewed exclusively in terms of performing a single role or function. Instead, individuals are seen as unique, complex and evolving; complete with hopes, dreams and personal history.

A shared vision exists when people recognize that they hold similar value systems. With a shared vision, members of the culture are enthusiastic about cultural goals and the processes by which they will be achieved. A shared vision implies a sense of inclusion: members of the culture are not being left behind.

A positive outlook, people look for opportunities rather than obstacles and for strengths rather than weaknesses in one another. It is not so much that the need for change is overlooked, but rather there is a general recognition that cultural and individual strengths will make it possible to improve upon current conditions.

Organizational Support Systems

There are a variety of mechanisms that define and perpetuate the culture. Formal structures such as laws, rules and policies play an important role. And informal structures such as the "grapevine" are also powerful. Information about organizational support can be organized into the following 10 broad categories: (1) modeling; (2) recruitment and selection; (3) orientation; (4) training; (5) rewards and recognition; (6) confrontation; (7) communication systems; (8) relationships and interactions; (9) symbols, myths and rituals; and (10) allocation of resources. Strengths and opportunities for improvement are identified for each of the 10 organizational support systems. When planning culture change, it can be helpful to utilize those aspects of existing organizational support systems that foster desired behaviour. The planning process must also be directed at changing those organizational support systems that work against project goals.

Peer Support

Family, friends and co-workers assist one another in a variety of ways. When most people think of peer support, they think about listening and advice giving. In its negative form such advice is sometimes called nagging. Other forms of peer support include modelling, eliminating barriers to change and celebrating success. Such support can be essential when people attempt to modify their personal behaviour. For this reason, the assessment of peer support systems is an important aspect of project planning.

Changing a Culture

The ever-fast changing business environment has made everything ephemeral in nature. So is organizational culture also. As organizations do not remain the same over a period of time, so is the case of culture as well. Culture established in one type of environment may not remain effective in changed environment. If it is so, the organization must either adapt to new conditions of environment or it may not survive. Hence, the need for change in organizational culture.

Among the major factors that create the right conditions for change in culture include:

A dramatic crisis: At times, there can be some shocks that undermine the *status quo* of culture and question its relevance in a new crisis. The examples of such crises might be a surprising financial setback, the loss of a major customer, or a dramatic technological breakthrough by a competitor which can change the market structure. For example, once the Maruti car was introduced in the Indian market, it shock up the otherwise sedate passenger car market, and forced other companies to take a more productive stance. Similarly, the economic reforms initiated during the 1990's, as well as the opening up of the global market, forced many companies to attempt changing their cultural orientation.

Change in Leadership

Changing top leadership can also have a major impact on organizational culture. New leadership at the organizational apex heralds signals of change. It will not be less than correct to say that the top leadership is the personification of the culture. This is because the top leadership sets the norms, values and formal reward system for achieving organizational goals. Many Indian companies like MMTC, SAIL and ACC, saw major changes occurring after new Chief Executive Officer (COEs) took over.

Creating a Culture

The founders start their organization with a vision on what their organization should be. Then, the vision is imposed on all organizational members. The members take in the vision through interaction and their own experience.

A distinct process involved in the creation of a culture—

1. A single person (founder) has an idea or vision for an enterprise.
2. The founder brings in some people and creates a core group that shares a common vision with the founder. All in the core group accept the idea or vision and work for it.
3. The founding core group begins to act in concert to create an organization by raising funds, obtaining patents, incorporating, locating space, building, and so on.

Almost all successful business firms are based on beliefs and value of past happening. It implies that the ultimate source of an organizations culture is it's founders starts their changes based on retaining and developing what is good in an existing culture and adding to its new elements that will stimulate progress therefore the skill reforming the culture of a company is to identify and retain the pride and honour in what is good while recognizing what is to be rejected or modified. At the same time the management of the firm should seek, generate new ideas and practices that can energies the firm and propel it forward with a new strength.

Enhancing Corporate Culture through 360-Degree Feedback

J. SRINIVASAN AND J. JAYAKUMAR

Performance appraisal has come to occupy a pivotal place in human resource function. The traditional merit rating which focused on personality traits was replaced by performance appraisal with focus on work results. In order to make appraisal more objective, transparent and participative, concepts such as self-appraisal, peer appraisal, subordinate appraisal and appraisal by customers both internal and external were introduced.

360-degree feedback is a process by which an individual gets his/her aggregated feedback from different categories of individuals—seniors (boss, reporting officer, reviewing officer), subordinates, direct and indirect reporters, peers (colleagues and internal customers), external customers and suppliers, and other role/set members with whom he/she is interacting.

The 360-degree feedback process involves collecting perceptions about a person's behaviour and the impact of that behaviour from the person's superiors, direct reports, colleagues, fellow members of project teams, internal and external customers, and suppliers. Multi-source feedback encourages openness and raises expectation, leading people to believe the organizational values, continuous learning and honesty. Most organizations appear to be using this process for:

- Leadership development (implementing their leadership models or reinforcing the same)
- Individual growth and development
- Competency building
- Enhance Corporate Culture
- Rarely or never for: Performance Appraisals, rewards and recognition, collecting data on employees, succession planning and career development.

CONSIDERATIONS BEFORE STARTING 360 DEGREE FEEDBACK

1. Purpose

It is important that people are clear about why this process is being used and what it is being used for. The purpose needs to be clearly and consistently communicated to all those involved.

2. Culture

Organizations need to consider whether the organizational culture supports this process and allows open feedback. The 360-degree feedback process relies heavily on the inputs of others so participants and raters need to feel comfortable and supported when taking part in this process.

3. Timing

Identifying when to introduce 360 degree feedback is an important consideration. It is not appropriate to introduce it during periods of downturn or when redundancies or re-organizations have been announced. During these periods, staffs are more likely to be feel threatened and concerned about the organization's intentions and therefore resistant to new feedback processes.

4. Roll out

Consider having a senior manager acting as a sponsor or champion of 360-degree feedback. This can greatly enhance its success and generate buy-in into the process. It is also important to involve staff as early as possible in the implementation of 360-degree feedback as it prevents secrecy and the feeling that this has been imposed on them.

5. Confidentiality

It is important to guarantee confidentiality for participants—both subjects and raters. Make sure the model you are using ensures this happens so that the feedback is not attributable to individual raters.

THE 360-DEGREE PROCESS

1. Self-assessment

Self-assessment encourages the individual to take responsibility for his or her own development and is a useful starting point in the 360-degree feedback process. Consideration needs to be given to the purpose of this information and how it is used as well as who has access to this data and how long is it held for.

2. The Raters

Identifying the most appropriate people to rate the performance of the individual is a key part of the process. Ideally the recipient will have full involvement in identifying who they think is in the best position to comment on their performance. The raters must be credible to the recipient for them to act on the resulting feedback.

2.1 Number of Raters

The assessment has to be based on a large enough sample to ensure that it is valid. If too small, there is a danger that one rater's view will have a major impact on the overall results. 7 to 12 respondents are usually sufficient in terms of reliability.

3. The Questionnaire

The design of the assessment, reporting and feedback process should suit the purpose of the exercise. It needs to describe the behaviours, which relate to actual job performance. It should relate to existing measurement systems within your area, such as competencies. It also needs to be in line with City's culture and values. The questionnaire needs to be relevant to the raters and their day-to-day involvement with the individual.

A well-designed questionnaire should offer respondents the opportunity to indicate where they have not had the opportunity to observe behaviour, or where the behaviour is not relevant to the job, so as not to force them to guess. Ideally the questionnaire should take between 15 and 30 minutes to complete.

3.1 Qualitative and Quantitative Data

The most effective questionnaire design is one that encompasses both quantitative as well as qualitative elements. The quantitative elements provide the structure and the qualitative questions provide the context.

4. Feedback Strategy

It is important to consider what feedback is communicated and how and when this takes place.

4.1 Feedback Report

Feedback usually consists of a report. The design of the report should be kept simple and ideally designed to help the individual priorities their relative strengths and development areas. Given that an individual is receiving sensitive information about how their colleagues, direct reports and manager view their performance, sensitivity is essential. Someone must be available to help interpret the results with that person.

4.2 Trained Facilitators

As 360-degree feedback is being used as part of the appraisal process, feedback is communicated face to face. The people giving the feedback (appraisers) must have had the relevant training to give them the skills to support this process.

4.3 When Feedback is Communicated

Ideally the individual receives feedback as soon as possible after that feedback has been collated. It is important to ensure that people receive it when there is support available to interpret the results, e.g. as part of a supportive appraisal process.

3. Evaluation

3.1 Purpose

Evaluating the impact of 360-degree feedback is an important part of determining its success. This is especially important if you have piloted this process and are considering rolling it out to other areas and/or are repeating the process.

3.2 Measures

Impact can be measured at both the organizational and individual level. This can include following up with participants about their views on the process as well as measuring the impact it had on their development plans. On an organizational level, monitoring key performance indicators will determine whether targets have been met more closely following the introduction of 360-degree feedback.

IMPLEMENTATION OF 360-DEGREE FEEDBACK PROCESS IN AN ORGANIZATION TO ENHANCE CORPORATE CULTURE

The internal working environment of every organization has certain commonly perceived psychological characteristics or traits which are collectively called its climate, culture or milieu. These traits generally vary from organization to organization, are relatively stable over time and influence the behaviour of people in the organization. Thus every organization has its own unique culture. Various personal characteristics such as values, attitudes, experience, etc., determine the manner in which members are likely to perceive the various aspects of internal working of their departments.

Benefits of 360-Degree Feedback

360-Degree feedback offers several advantages. Some of these include:

Benefits to Corporates

- It provides a more objective and acceptable feedback.
- Very effective for developing leadership and other competencies considered critical for performing various Leadership and Managerial roles effectively.
- Serves as a team-building tool as it is more involving and participative.
- Promotes a culture of openness.
- Promotes total quality with emphasis on internal and external customer orientation.
- Results in better quality of HR decisions for training and rewards.
- Helps in identification of competency gaps and planning development interventions.
- It is a good supplement to normal appraisals but not a substitute to them.

Benefits to the Individual

- Serves as a team-building tool as it is more involving and participative.
- Helps to ascertain if your impact on others within the organization is in the desired manner/direction.
- Enhances self-awareness.
- Helps discover strengths, weaknesses and blind spots.
- Provides direction for change and development.
- Focuses attention on actions and behaviours valued by others; thereby improving work relations.

- Helps discover areas where you have not yet made a significant impact.

INGREDIENTS FOR THE SUCCESS OF 360-DEGREE FEEDBACK IN AN ORGANIZATION

360-degree feedback systems can be very sensitive. A person who is not well prepared for it can be thrown out of balance. If not designed and conducted well, it has the potential danger of developing wrong perceptions or notions. It is therefore necessary and important to manage the process well and make it foolproof. The first important step is to determine if the organization is ready for it. The second important step is to determine if thc candidate is ready for it.

The following are the indicators of an organization's readiness for 360-Degree Feedback:

- The top management of the organization is committed to develop the competencies of employees on a continuous basis.
- HRD systems operating in the organization being taken seriously in implementation.
- The top management is willing to invest their time and effort in giving feedback to their own subordinates.
- The top management is adequately committed to competency building through 360-Degree Feedback.
- People take feedback supportively and use it for development.
- The organization already is or is in the process of becoming a customer-driven organization.
- The HRD department has a high degree of credibility.

The following are indicators to assess the readiness of a candidate for the 360-Degree Feedback:

- The candidate has a desire to know himself through the eyes of others.
- The candidate desire to be better.
- The candidate should be a learning-oriented individual.

- The candidate is receptive and respects the views of others.

TVRLS Experience with 360-Degree Feedback

TVRLS has covered over 3000 top-level managers so far from various organizations involving around 30,000 assessors. Research conducted by them to study the effectiveness of 360-degree feedback in enhancing overall effectiveness of top and senior management shows the following predominant changes:

They begin to focus more on leadership roles such as:

- Articulating vision and sharing it more systematically.
- Spending more time on communicating vision and goals.
- Being more developmental as against benevolent or critical.
- Paying more attention to and showing concern for individual needs rather than being preoccupied with one's own ideas and issues.

Enhanced Internal customer orientation, which is indicated by:

- Better interaction with colleagues and subordinates.
- Learning from colleagues and benefiting from their experiences.
- Building better rapport with seniors.

Increased focus on fostering team spirit which gets reflected in terms of:

- Setting high goals for the team.
- More participative management.
- Better conflict management.
- Higher mutuality and more receptive to feedback.
- Increased sensitivity to others' feelings.
- Creating a more collaborative culture.
- Cross-functional review mechanism getting instituted.

Marked increase in delegation and subordinates' development in terms of:

- Empowering subordinates to take higher responsibilities.
- Leaving routine decisions to lower levels.
- Not interfering in matters being handled by subordinates.
- Encouraging subordinates to learn from their mistakes and being patient with them.

Predominant behavioural changes have been reported in terms of:

- Becoming assertive.
- Clear communication.
- Higher initiative.
- Being more patient.
- Being more proactive.
- Better time management.

In terms of the impact on their unit/department/organization, participants who responded felt that the changes they demonstrated post-feedback, have generated increased motivation especially among their subordinates. In addition, increased sensitivity to their managerial and leadership roles has resulted in better working relationships and, a more congenial atmosphere.

Drawbacks

Not every process is perfect and 360-degree feedback programs are no exception. Subordinates may rate bosses high because they are afraid of retaliation. Peers tend to evaluate each other's positively well, perhaps to avoid disrupting the group. On the other hand, peers tend to rate their colleagues on the lower side. Nevertheless, the number of people and variety of perspectives involved in a 360-degree feedback process should ensure a generally unbiased and accurate view of a person's performance.

A 360-degree feedback process in an organization gathers information, usually through a questionnaire, about the performance of employees or managers from people all around them—including peers, subordinates and even customers. This type of multi-perspective evaluation is more complete and accurate than the traditional top-down evaluation. Superiors only see a portion of a manger's performance. They need other perspectives to fill in the blanks. Subordinates can provide important information on the leadership qualities of a manager. Customers are in a better position, than anyone, to evaluate how employees perform with customers.

A 360-degee feedback evaluation is also valuable because people do not act the same toward everyone. The interpersonal skills of a manager are probably more accurately reflected in feedback from subordinates or peers than in feedback from a manger's superiors.

Another important aspect of 360-degree feedback is the inclusion of self-evaluations. Ratings by others will probably be more accurate, but self-evaluations force employees and managers to sit down and think about their strength and weakness.

Finally, 360-degree feedback evaluations have the advantage of confidentiality. Top-down evaluations are usually not confidential. Supervisors must be prepared to defend their evaluations, which may cause them to soften or in some way alter what they might have said anonymously. Since 360-degree feedback involves groups of raters, the results are anonymous.

Organizational Values, Vision and Culture

M.A. KRISHNAMURTHY

VALUE

According to economist Milton Friedman, there is only one value to be maximized, namely profit other values are protected by the rules of society. Thus, Friedman acknowledges implicitly that there are several stakeholders in a firm, but decision-makers need only pay attention to one. The preferred stakeholder: the owner, the underlying belief being that the mechanisms of the free market will automatically maximize the welfare of the others.

The organization as a voluntary meeting place of actors that have come together to provide their resources to create value.

Shareholders provide Equity,
Workers provide Skills and Labour,
Consumers provide Revenue,

Suppliers provide Physical Resources, and
The local Community provides Infrastructure, etc.

All stakeholders expect value back for what they provide. Thus, Return on Investment, Worker's Salary, Quality Goods, Business and Work Places are examples of values that are created.

These are identified three different value categories:

- *Core Values*—These values prescribe behaviour, and tell the character and attitude of the organization.
- *Created Values*—These are the values the stakeholders have come together to produce and are the raison debenture for the organization, the distribution of such values is subject to trade-off by decision-makers or bargaining processes.
- *Protected Values*—These values are not supposed to suffer infringement. Trade-off against other values is considered unethical and management protects them through rules, standards and regulations.

The three value categories differ in two important respects, namely with regard to ethics and emotionality.

Value System

Core Values	*Created Values*	*Protected Values*
• Pioneering Spirit	• Stake holders	• Health Values
• Respect	• Owners	• Safety Values
• Commitment	• Stock Value	Environmental
• Trust Worthiness	• Dividends	Values and
• Agility	*Customers*	Missions
• Responsibility	• Energy	
• Capability	Community	
• Accountability	Citizenship	

The importance of values in the formation of visions and they outline three vision formation processes built on this idea:

- The Intuitive Approach—is primarily based on structured introspection.
- The Analytic Approach—focuses on gathering information from various Individuals about the direction of the organization.
- The Benchmarking Approach—looks to the Competition for standards and creates a vision based on subsequent finding.

Vision

In conducting this review, two topics that often appeared in conjunction with organizational vision included organizational mission and visionary leadership.

Mclean, noted that there is not a commonly accepted distinction between mission and vision, and then clarified that "mission. Refers to the organizations purpose or reason for being" and "Vision is a statement of how the organizations would like to look at some time in the future and includes the values and philosophy for which it would like to be known".

Vision is, therefore, the picture of the future that the company wants to achieve. An organizational vision is an opportunity for organizations to uniquely define themselves. Vision plays a significant role in strategic management and strategic planning. Vision could be meaningless if employees do not embrace it and use it to guide decision-making.

Organizational Vision consists of three main factors, including:

- The guiding beliefs and principles of the organization,
- The enduring organizational purpose that grows out of these beliefs, and
- A catalyzing mission that is consistent with organizational purpose while moving the organizational towards the achievements of that purpose.

Vision is often considered part of the strategic process within organizations. Each vision has a core and at that core should be the focus of products, services, markets, organizations, or ideals. With strategy in mind, this core is referred to as the strategic content and one goal should be to add value to the organization. Strategy is the path that an organization chooses to pursue its future, while vision should describe a future in which "goals and strategy are being successfully achieved in lockstep with the organizations guiding philosophy and values".

A vision should be brief, verifiable, focused, understandable to all employees and inspirational.

Implementation required either an extremely clear and meaningful vision, or someone who can decode the vision statement and translate it into meaningful parts.

Implementing a vision is different from implementing something like a training program because a vision is more ambiguous and often does not necessarily have clearly defined start and end points.

Effective communication within organizations is a key to vision implementation. Whether the vision is accepted or rejected by employees, stakeholders and the general public.

For effective implementation must translate the vision form words to pictures with a vivid description of what it will be like to achieve their goal.

Individual perception of vision is important because it is the individuals within the organization who actually put the vision into action.

Related considerations might include ensuring that employees understand the vision, clarifying what the vision means in regard to each individual position within the organization, and making sure that the resources to execute the vision are in place.

Making these things happen requires much planning and thought to assure that the human resources are available and prepared to carry out the implementation.

IMPLICATIONS FOR HUMAN RESOURCE DEVELOPMENT

Vision development, Vision content Selection and Vision implementation each require careful planning, and HRD can play an important role in maximizing the effectiveness of each of these phases. HRD roles vary across organizations, so in order to influence all three phases of the vision process HRD must first be in a strategic position to do so.

Culture

Culture is often associated with exotic, distant peoples and places, with myths, rites, foreign languages and practices. Researchers have observed that within our own society, organization members. Similarly engaged in rituals, pass along corporate myths and stories, and use arcane jargon and that these informal practices may foster or hinder management's goal for the organization.

Culture as "the shared philosophies, ideologies, values, assumption, beliefs, expectation, attitudes and norms".

It is a system of shared values (what is important) and beliefs (how things work) that interact with a company's people, organizational structures and control systems to produce behavioural norms".

It is the pattern of shared values and beliefs that help individuals understand organizational functioning and thus provide them with norms for behaviour in the organization.

Employees are often strongly committed to the shared cultural values of the organization. The way that the organization functions may be determined by these values.

For instance, the organization usually makes public pronouncement about its culture in the form of a mission statement or code of ethics, or a statement of aspirations.

The buildings and physical workspace will give visible evidence of the culture. Organizational structure, management style, corporate rituals and procedures and HR systems such as recruitment and promotion, will all reflect the entrenched cultural values. Employees will have chosen to join and remain in the organization because they actively support the practiced culture and will therefore be extremely resistant to change.

Similarly, senior management may choose to perpetuate the *status quo* by promoting managers who will continue the current culture.

Promoting from within provides a stability and certainly which the majority of employees prefer. If a new chief executive is appointed from outside the organization, he or she may attempt to change the culture to mirror his or her chosen philosophies and values.

However, this may prove very difficult, and it is offer the case that the chief executive may change and adapt to the existing culture, or there may be a gradual melding of the two sets of values.

Symbols are the first layer of the onion to be revealed,
Heroes are the second layer of the onion, and
Rituals are the third layer of the onion.

Symbols include words, gestures, pictures and objects. They are easily visible to people outside the culture. Symbols are the most visible components of culture.

Heroes are people living or dead, real or imaginary who serve as models of behaviour.

Rituals are collective activities, technically superfluous in reaching desired ends, but considered as socially essential within a culture.

Values are the core of national culture and are the broad tendencies for preference of certain states of affairs over others.

Organizational values are based on the objectives of the organization, vision and mission are integral part of the implementation of the organization policy for the accomplishment of organizational culture providing a framework within which the policies can be implemented and organizational goals can be achieved. Value, Vision and Culture form an integral part of HR polices and HRD.

Impact of Corporate Cultures on Effectiveness

T. Afsar Basha

It has been proved by umpteen studies that success and failures of the organizations is mostly due to its own culture, even though other factors like marketing, finance, planning, production, etc. acts as facilitators. Corporate culture has become an important tool for the executives to introduce and manage organizational change. They realized that significant strategic or structural alignment couldn't occur if the organization's values and behavioural norms do not support it. Organizations create and indoctrinate certain basic values and assumptions that drive the organizational members to go together. These beliefs and assumptions may operate at conscious and unconscious levels. Studies have found amazing results on the impact of organizational culture on their productivity and over all effectiveness of the organization. The research works by various behavioural scientists (like Thomas J. Peters and Robert H. Waterman, William Ouchi, etc.) have proved that highly successful companies in America have the similarities of Japanese Culture. Many other studies (like Edger H. Schein, Payne, L.) have also contributed to the belief that corporate culture is a highly significant factor and real contributor to the success of the organizations. In India comparing to western countries only a few studies (like Jai B.P. Sinha, Anup Kumar Singh, Saiyadain) have concentrated on the aspect of organizational culture and organizational effectiveness.

A NEW HUMANISTIC APPROACH

The impact of organizational culture both in India and Western countries have either adopted or developed certain patterns of organizational cultures which are organizational specific and totally depended organizational factors rather than individual factors. These studies approached the organizational culture through organizational dimensions such as leadership styles, organizational structures, centralization, delegation, etc. and have completely marginalized and neglected the individual's dimensions. Hence, these studies are lacking clarity and contradicting in themselves. Further these studies have failed to point out exactly which pattern or typology of culture leads to either success or failure.

The fundamental assumption in organizational psychology is that it is impossible to understand the behaviour in organization, without understanding the characteristics, behaviour of individuals operating within organizations. Based on current knowledge and conceptual developments in the field of human psychology, it should no longer be acceptable to treat culture as somehow opposed to or independent of human nature. And it should no longer be acceptable to ignore evolutionary psychological foundation through which culture is created and transmitted. It is also unreasonable to expect that human culture deviate from its foundations when it enters organizations. Therefore, corporate culture cannot be discussed in isolation from the totality of the human nature.

Now with this background, a maiden attempt has been made to study both effectiveness and ineffectiveness of an organization based on their culture patterns. This study departs from other studies in terms of the typologies developed on the basis of humanistic psychoanalysis. This study uses two typologies, i.e. Progressive and Regressive for identifying the cultural patterns of an organization.

PROGRESSIVE CULTURE

Progressive culture is a combination of innovation and emotional orientation. It includes basic elements of innovation, emotional fondness, personal relations, positive stroking, etc. Innovation is the basic element of progressive culture. Progressiveness can be brought to the organization only through innovations. Innovative organization fosters the spirit of competitiveness, which ultimately leads to success. In the present scenario of corporate world, the term "innovation" is not only a way of business but it has become a lifeline for the existence and survival of the industry. Technological changes are taking place rapidly throughout the world. In order to keep pace with the development, the organizations should be innovative; otherwise they will be thrown out from map of business world. Now the slogan of the organization is "Innovate or Perish". The future belongs to those organizations, who are able infuse innovativeness in their organizations.

Dimensions of Progressive Culture

Progression is not like most other business functions and activities. There are no reliable rules, processes and templates or even measures of progression. Progression has to be brought in each and every activities of the organization. It may be for the development of innovation or development of personnel relations or new products or for some new ways of working or new marketing strategies or even entirely new lines of business. Therefore, there is no standard procedures or tools to promote progressive culture in organization.

As mentioned earlier, we cannot expect a general, universally accepted formula or framework to foster progressive culture in the organizations. But based on the findings of research studies of most successful and innovative organizations predominant values of progressive culture.

Strong belief in being the best, strong belief in the importance of details of execution, strong belief in the importance of people as individuals, strong belief in superior quality and service, strong belief that most members of the organization should be innovators, strong belief in supporting failures, strong belief in the importance of informality, strong belief in and recognition of the importance of economic growth and profits, emphasis on improvisation rather than forecasting, Emphasis on opportunities rather than constraints emphasis on cooperation rather than competition, discovering new actions rather than defending past actions, Encouraging doubts and contradictions over blind belief, Value arguments more highly than serenity, High rate of participation and involvement, High rate of commitment to technology, High rate of commitment to quality and perfectionism.

All the above-mentioned characteristics can be brought under 8 dimensions. Presence of these dimensions in an organization will indicate the presence of progressive culture. To simplify and facilitate further, all these 8 dimensions are made to start with alphabet "E" and named "8 E's" approach to progressive culture. Following are these "8 E" dimensions.

Effectiveness: Includes characteristics like goal setting, goal attainment, bias towards action, growth focus, maximization of output and profits, etc.

Efficiency: Includes quality consciousness, perfectionism, optimum utilization of resources, tolerance for mistakes and failures, aligning innovation with business objectives etc.,

Execution: Consists·intensity of execution, to which extent plans are executed, receptivity and adaptability of new ideas, integration of personal and organizational objectives, etc.

Empowerment: Consists of autonomy, delegation of powers and allocation of resources to innovative ideas; recognition of informality in organization, involvement and participation of the field level workers in decision-making, etc.,

Excellence: Organizational values such as—emphasis on opportunities rather than constraints, emphasis on improvisation rather than forecasting, encouraging doubts and contradictions over blind belief. Value arguments more highly than serenity, fostering cooperation rather than competition.

Efforts: Efforts of management to develop abilities, risk-taking, fighting negativity, developing optimism, supporting failures, recognition of informality, technology upgradation, etc.,

Enthusiasm: Management interest in—recognition of high performers, performance link rewards system, motivating innovative ideas, simultaneous—loose and tight approach, financial and other support to innovative ideas and innovators, establishment of innovation club, etc.

Expertise: Management willingness—in upgradation of technology—hiring even outsiders to bring expertise, availing professionals help, consultancy services, establishment of R&D cells, budgetary allocations for R&D, etc.

Organizational Culture

R. Rangarajan and R. Usha

Inside the organization lies a powerful force for determining individual and group behaviour. Organization culture is the set of assumptions, belief, values and norms that are shared by an organization's members. This culture may have been consciously created by its key member, or it may have simply evolved across time. It represents a key element of the work environment in which employees perform their jobs. This idea of organizational culture is somewhat intangible, for we cannot see it or touch it, but it is present and pervasive. Like air in the room, it surrounds and affects everything that happens in an organization. Because it is a dynamic system concept, culture is also affected by everything that happens within an organization.

Organization culture is important to a firm for several reasons. They give an organizational identity to employees—a defining vision of what the organization represents. They are also an important source of stability and continuity to the organization, which provides a sense of security to its members. At the same time, knowledge of organizational culture helps newer employees interpret that goes on inside the organization, by providing an important context for event that would otherwise seem confusing. More than anything else, perhaps, culture helps stimulate employee's enthusiasm for their tasks. Cultures attract attention, convey a vision, and typically honor high-producing and creative individuals as heroes. By recognizing and rewarding these people, organization cultures are identifying them as role models to emulate.

LEVELS OF ORGANIZATION CULTURE

It suggested that organization culture can exist on several levels which may vary in terms of visibility and resistance to change.

The various levels of organization culture includes:

Shared assumptions: These are the deepest level of organization culture representing beliefs about human nature and realities which are taken for granted.

Cultural values: These represent collective beliefs, values, assumption and feeling about what things are good, normal, valuable, etc. and have a tendency to persist over a period of time even when organizational membership changes.

Shared behaviours: These refer to those norms which are more visible and easier to change as compared to values.

Cultural symbols: This is the most superficial level of organizational culture which may consist of symbols—words, gestures, pictures or other physical objects which convey a particular meaning within a culture.

DIMENSIONS OF ORGANIZATIONAL CULTURE

Following are the dimensions of the organizational culture:

Supervision is the extent to which supervisors maintain good relations with their subordinate, offer them socio-economic support and help in improving their skills and chances of advancement.

Management of reward is the extent to which rewards are

related to performance and required system of behaviour in the organization.

Communication is the extent of flow of information in the different directions and its mode (formal or informal).

Trust is who is trusted by management and to what extent? What is the extent of inter-personal trust?

Decision-making is who makes decision: whether people high in the hierarchy or those involved in the matter?

Problem management is how are problems viewed—as irritants or as challenges 'how are they handled'?

Innovation and changes is who initiate changes? How change and innovation are perceived? How change is implemented.

DETERMINANT OF ORGANIZATION CULTURE

Factors which influence the above dimensions of OC are as under.

Economic Condition

An organization's economic climate influences its climate in several ways. The more prosperous an organization is, the more it can afford to spend on research and innovation and the more it can afford to take risk and be adventurous.

Leadership Style

An organization leadership style plays a profound role in determining several aspects of its culture. Thus, an authoritarian style may make the organization's culture characterized by high position structure, low individual autonomy, low reward orientation, low warmth and support and so on. Opposite may be the culture characteristics of an organization with democratic leadership style.

Organizational Policies

OC is also influenced by organizational policies. A policy to resort to layoff only as a last remedy during business downturn will foster a cordial and supportive climate. Similarly, a policy to reward employees for increase in profit will make culture more reward-oriented.

Employee's Characteristics

An organization with educated, ambitious and young employees is likely have a different type of OC than what may be expected of an organization whose Employees have opposite characteristics. The former set of characteristics may foster a competitive, risk-taking and open climate.

Organizational Size

Small organizations with few levels of management are generally more amenable to democratic and participative functioning than big organizations. Systems of communication are also more open in small organizations. Hence these organizations foster a different type of climate than what one comes across in big organizations.

DEVELOPMENT OF ORGANIZATION CULTURE

Culture creation can be the outcome of certain critical values or using leaders as a model for imbibing values into the work. Or it can be said that the organization culture is formed in response to two types of challenges which can confront an organization. These may take the form of: (1) External adaptation and survival, and (2) Internal integration.

External Adaptation and Survival

External adaptation and survival reveals how the organization will strive to create a niche in and cope with the constantly changing external environment. Specifically stated it means addressing the following issues:

Vision, Mission and Strategy

What I the long-term vision of the organization? What is the primary purpose of its existence? How strategic decisions are made to pursue the 'vision and mission'.

Goals

Working out specific targets which are to be achieved.

Means

Determine how the goals are achieved through designing a suitable organization structure and reward system.

Measurement

Establishing criteria to measure how well individuals and groups are accomplishing their goals.

Internal Integration

This refers to the establishment and maintenance of effective working relationship among the members of the organization. Internal integration calls for addressing the following issues:

Languages and Concept Development

Identify the language (and methods) for communicating and developing a shared meaning for important concepts.

Group and Team Boundaries

Establishing criteria for membership and team activities.

Power and Status

Work out the rules for acquiring, maintaining and losing power and status.

Rewards and Punishments

Develop organization system to encourage and promote desirable (ethical) behaviour and discourage undesirable behaviour.

In the beginning, i.e. when the organization is run by the founder(s)—it will be these individual(s) who may influence the organization culture.

Thus the new organization can also emerge either a new (or younger) member(s) join the organization and bring with them new knowledge and assumptions as they develop and identify ways to cope with issues of external adaptation and internal integration. Of course, the national culture, customs, rituals, and social norms of the country can also shape and influence the organizational culture.

MAINTAINING ORGANIZATIONAL CULTURE

Ways in which organization operate and are manages will have significant influence on maintaining and changing organizational culture. It can be said that organizational culture to the great extent will be dependent upon the individuals who fit into its culture and the maintaining of its culture can be done by removing employees who are not able to behave in accordance to the company's accepted behaviour and norms. The following are some of the powerful re-enforcers of an organizational culture.

The process and behaviour noticed and paid attention to by employees, teams and managers:

One of the most powerful methods of maintaining organization culture is the involvement of the processes and behaviours or events that are paid attention to and commented upon sending strong signals about what is expected of them.

Handling of Crisis and Incidents

When the organization faces a crisis, the manner in which the crisis is dealt with, will reveal a lot about the organization culture-either reinforce the existing or bring out new values and norms that can change the culture in some way.

Role Modeling, Training and Guidance

Various aspects of the organizational culture are also revealed by the way managers perform their roles—organizational culture massages are clearly incorporated into the corporate training programmed and day-to-day functioning, coaching and guiding on the job.

The Method for Rewarding Performance

The organization's method(s) for rewarding and punishing behaviours of employees help to communicate to employees the priorities and values of both individual managers and the organization. Similarly, organization's status system—

distribution of perk, type of executive and manager chamber, employee's dining room, recreation facilities will demonstrate and reveal a lot about the roles and behaviours most valued by the organization.

The Recruitment and Selection Process

The method of recruiting clearly reveals the criteria used to determine who is assigned to specific jobs or position, how and when certain people are give increments and promotions, what is the practice followed for early retirement or removal from the job and so on will speak about the organizational culture.

Organizational Rites and Ceremonies

Organizational rites and ceremonies are planned managerial or employee's activities or rituals, over a period of time can easily be interpreted as part of organizational culture. These could take the form of rites of passage (facilitates transition into new role), rites of degradation (to reaffirm proper behaviour, reduce power and perks), etc. Ceremonies could take the form of award functions to facilitate the best achievers, etc., such ceremonies tend to increase the identity and status of high performing employees as well as emphasize the company's reward for excellence. Similarly, ceremonies will reveal the many of the underlying beliefs and values of an organization which are expressed in the form of stories and become a part of its folklore.

IMPACT OF CULTURE ON ORGANIZATIONAL EFFECTIVENESS

Impact of culture on organization's effectiveness is both functional and dysfunctional.

Negative Impact

Talking about the latter, it may be stated that culture leads to, resistance to change, resistance to diversity, barrier to acquisition and merger. Now let us understand this in detail,

Barrier to Change

Culture is liability when the shared values are not in agreement with those that will further the organization's effectiveness. This is most likely to occur when the organization's environment is dynamic. When an environment is undergoing rapid change, an organization's entrenched culture may no longer be appropriate. So consistency of behaviour is an asset to an organization when it faces a stable environment. It may, however, burden the organization and make it difficult to respond to change in the environment.

Barrier to Diversity

Organizations seek out and hire diverse individuals because of the alternative strengths these people bring to the workplace. Yet these diverse behaviours and strengths are likely to diminish in strong culture as people attempts to fit in. Strong cultures therefore, can be liabilities when they effectively eliminate the unique strength that the people of different backgrounds bring to the organization. Moreover, strong culture can also be liability when they support institutional bias or become insensitive to people who are different.

Barriers to Acquisition and Merger

Historically the key factors that management looked at in making acquisition or merger decisions were related to financial advantage or product synergy. In the recent years, cultural compatibility has become the primary concern. While a favourable financial statement or product line may be the initial attraction of an acquisition candidate, whether the acquisition actually works seems to have more to do with how well the two organization's culture match up. A number of acquisitions consummated in the 1990s have already failed and the primary cause is conflicting organizational culture.

Positive Impact

On the positive side, culture has an impact on control, normative order, innovation promotion, and employee performance and satisfaction.

Effective Control

Organizational culture serves as a control mechanism in directing behaviour. As the culture is diffused throughout the organization, people understand what they are supposed to do and what they are not should not do. When individuals are not in accordance with the beliefs and values of the culture, managers and co-workers will step in and insist on corrective action. A strong culture is characterized by shared beliefs and expectations to which all must adhere.

Innovation Promotion

Cultures promote innovation. Organizations develop norms such as risk-taking, reward for changes and openness that promote such activity.

Normative Order

Closely linked to effective control is the use of norms to guide behaviours. These expectations regarding appropriate and inappropriate behaviors are greatly influenced by culture and strong culture have both consensus and intensity regarding these norms.

Everyone understands the culturally based norms and there is strong support for them. In weak cultures, consensus may be present but intensity is not. This comparison helps explain why some organizations are successful at what they do. It also helps explain why organizations with strong cultures often have great difficulty changing their strategies and behaviours. The norms that dictate these actions have been reinforced so strongly that the personnel are reluctant to abandon them in favour of other behaviours.

Performance and Satisfaction

Organizational culture has its impact on performance and satisfaction of organizational members, but not in equal proportions. There is relatively strong relationship between culture and satisfaction, but this is moderated by individual needs and culture. In general, satisfaction will be the highest when there is congruence between the needs and the culture.

Thus, job satisfaction often varies according to the employee's perception of organization's culture.

It is said that culture and performance are interrelated, but the relationship seems to be less clear. In any case, the relationship is moderated by the organization's technology. If the culture is informal, creative risk-taking and conflict, performance will be higher if the technology is non-routine. The more formally structured organizations that are risk aversive, that seek to eliminate conflict, and that are prone to more task oriented leadership will achieve higher performance when routine technology is utilized. Socialization also has influence on performance.

CULTURAL AUDITS

Mangers must understand and monitor their organization's current culture to develop and effectively manage it. Thus, a cultural audit should be conducted periodically. This type of audit is an analysis designed to uncover shared values and beliefs in an organization.

The following four steps may be used in conducting a cultural audit.

Analyze the process and content of the socialization of a new associates and managers (interview those directly involved in socialization).

Analyze responses to critical incidents in the organization's history (construct an organizational biography from documents and interviews of past and present associates and managers.

Analyze the values and beliefs of culture creators (founder) and carriers (current leaders) (observe and/or interview the founders and current leaders).

Explore anomalies or puzzling features discovered in other analysis (initiate joint problem-solving sessions with current leaders in the organization).

A cultural audit is a complex and lengthy process that should be conducted only after careful planning and preparation. The results of an audit might indicate a culture that is not well developed or might disclose the presence of sub-cultures. An underdeveloped culture poses less of a problem than that is dysfunctional, fully developed, and self-reinforcing, because the less developed culture can be more easily influenced and its path altered if necessary.

- The organization should take steps to make necessary procedures for the communication of business plans.
- For good interpersonal relationship between the employees of different departments, it is necessary that these departments in the organization should work in a coordinated manner.
- Necessary steps should be taken by the organization to empower them to make decisions on behalf of their superiors.
- The organization should take necessary steps to develop self-managed teams for team orientation.
- For cordial relations between the superiors and subordinates work should be delegated by the superiors to his subordinates.
- HR department should take necessary steps to find top talent among diverse groups for the better employee satisfaction in the organization.

Organizational Culture : Make or Break the Company

N. Md. Faiyas Ahmed

Organizational culture is a powerful phenomenon. Why? Because it can literally make or break a company, deciding the difference between its success and failure. A strong organizational culture is one of the hardest things a business can build and successfully keep. The reason most businesses work towards it is because it really does improve the business. Culture is a powerful element that shapes your work enjoyment, your work relationships, and your work processes. But, culture is something that you cannot actually see, except through its physical manifestations in your work place. In many ways, culture is like personality. In a person, the personality is made up of the value, beliefs, underlying assumptions, interests, experiences, upbringing, and habits that create a person's behaviour.

Assess Your Organizational Culture

You can assess your current organizational culture in several ways. Participate in a culture walk: one-way to observe the culture in your organization is to take a walk around the building, and look at some of the physical signs of culture. Look around. What do the headquarters and other buildings look like? How is the space allocated? Where are the offices located? How much space is given to whom? Where are people located? What is posted on bulletin boards or displayed on walls? What is displayed on desks or in other areas of the building? In the work groups? On lockers or closets? How common areas utilized? What do people write to one another? What is said in memos or email? What the tone is of messages (formal or informal, pleasant or hostile, etc.)? How often do people communicate with one another? Is all communication written, or do people communicate verbally? What interaction between employees do you see? How much emotion is expressed during the interaction?

Culture Interviews: Another way to understand the culture of your organization is to interview your employees is small groups. It is just as important, during these interviews to observe the behaviours and interaction patterns of people, as it is to hear what they say about the culture. Since it is usually difficult for people to put into words what the culture is like, indirect questions will gain the most information. The following are examples of indirect questions you can ask during a culture interview:

What would you tell a friend about your organization if he or she was about to start working here?

What is the one thing you would most like to change about this organization?

Who is a hero around here? Why?

What is your favourite characteristic that is present in your company?

What kinds of people fail in your organization?

What is your favourite question to ask a candidate for a job in your company?

How are people dressed? How much interaction is there? Who is talking to whom? How does the place "feel"?

Read newsletter and other internal documents. What values are emphasized? Who is help up for praise? Are parties, celebrations, or other ceremonies mentioned? What sorts of things are discussed?

See what you can learn about rites and ceremonies in the organization. What happens when people accomplish something? Are there "rites of passage" such as promotion ceremonies and retirement parties? Are there regular "get-togethers" such as holiday parties, social events, and company softball games?

Warning Signs

You may hear less laughter in the office or notice that people seem unfocused. Employees may begin working shorter days, taking longer lunches or even asking for more compensation. When employees request additional compensation, it usually means that they're revaluating their contributions to your company's goals or mission.

ORGANIZATIONAL CULTURE IN DIFFERENT COMPANIES

Infosys

Infosys Technologies Ltd., (NASDAQ: INFY), a world leader in consulting and information technology services, partners with Global 2000 companies to provide business consulting, systems integration, application development and product engineering services.

There are three dimensions of the work culture at Infosys. The physical environment—is quit outstanding, the social and cultural does gives the feeling of belonging and most importantly the work ethic which provides the opportunity to perform and the recognition for performance. The attitude of management towards their employees is the key factor here. Here is a company that gives prime importance to its employees who they think are the main people because of which the company is where it is.

This is one company which believes in providing everything in-house. They are not satisfied with just having a few buildings for running their operations. The most common things that anyone can find in any of the Infosys DCs (Development Centres) are cool buildings designed which look like architectural wonders, swimming pool, Gymnasium, 2 to 3 Food courts, Café Coffee day outlets, Domino Pizza outlet, in some cases a departmental store and employees care center also known as the infy hostel which is actually like a four-star hotel and many more things and these are present in all the Infosys DCs. These are some of the things that motivate the people to work here.

The work culture here in Infosys is really good. Here employees call each other by their first name and no suffixes like Sir, Ma'am etc., are to be put neither prefixes like Mr. Ms. etc., are preferred. Also the seating arrangement does not showcase the level of authority and everyone is treated like one. Employee and their superior stand in the same line while taking lunch at the food court.

The company, an extension of the family, takes care of every individual's need, from seeing an employee through a close relative's illness to celebrating special occasions together. A number of social events are organized regularly where both the employees and their families participate. Besides other programmes, an annual special day 'Petit Infoscion" is held where the children of employees participate and have an opportunity to explore their parents' workplace.

Life at Infosys is brimming with events—where employees can pursue their interests in areas as varied as arts, culture or sports. The objective is to ensure that employees are not confined to their desks. Employees express their various skills and interests through forums that include an "Art Gallery" on campus dedicated to displaying the work of "Infoscions", daily quiz competitions, and regular meetings that keep the place abuzz with creativity.

"InSync is an internal communication program focused on keeping the Infoscion abreast of latest corporate and business developments, and equipping him or her to be a "brand ambassador" for the company. This program combines a communication portal with workshops, monthly newsletters, articles, daily cartoons and brainteasers to synchronize each Infoscion with the organization.

Infosys have a 'leadership training' institute in Mysore where they are grooming next generation leaders for Infosys. It is more of a systematic approach where the leaders are 'grooming inside'. Because of this reason it is very hard to see people quitting Infosys.

Infosys excels in promoting an acceptable and respectable method of communication. The only thing which works here is one-to-one communication behind close doors. No shouting at anyone, no pinpointing anyone in front of the rest of the crowd. This does provide for a healthier outlook with confident employees who don't have to do away with their self-respect. The hierarchy is always maintained and there is enough professionalism in the air. You are provided with a lot of room to add value to your own life. If you need a mentor, your immediate boss or someone higher up is always there to provide you with useful advice.

Nokia

Nokia Corporation is a manufacturer of mobile devices. Nokia offers consumers a range of mobile devices. The company also provides equipment, solutions and services for network operators, service providers and corporations. Nokia operates through four business groups: Mobile Phones, Multimedia, Enterprise Solutions and Networks. A flat, networked organization along with speed and flexibility in decision-making characterized Nokia's culture. Nokia believed in providing equal opportunities to people. The company had attempted to shape a culture of respect, openness and trust. Here everybody helped each other out, no matter what the situation. Individuals have a great deal of responsibility and freedom to make independent decisions. This approach gives a sense of trust, which is needed in our team-oriented way of working.

At Nokia, a lot of efforts are taken to ensure that every employee knows and understands the company's strategies and goals. This helps keep employees committed and inspired. Knowing the BIG picture helps people set and achieve their own goals, be truly accountable and feel empowered in their work. They offer fitness facilities and programs as well as other sporting, social and cultural activities, which promote workplace relationships as well as personal development and comport. These well-being services may also include laundry service, cafeteria, take-away food, day care and on-site caretaker services. It provides the opportunities for personal growth and responsibilities. They emphasize on informal culture and treat every employee as their family members, all employees are treated equally.

Improving organizational culture has become a necessity in today's ever-changing business environment. People want to work for a company where they can be happy and balance work and life. Organizations that treat their members well have experienced a better retention rate, an increased productivity and a happier overall culture. Improving organizational culture can be a big challenge for the organization and its members.

The Importance of Organizational Values

C.S. VIJAYA

Values have recently become more prominent in the commercial world. Research in business organizations is notoriously poor, because it often uses little other than correlational evidence, without any controls or attempts to establish causality. Nevertheless, several studies over the past decade have indicated how powerful an organization's values can be improving its performance.

It has been proved that many numbers of companies had outperformed their competitors over many years. They considered several possibilities but showed that the companies that were successful in the long-term were strongly.oriented to values. They had a strongly ethical culture that supported predetermined and declared values. It has been noted that company's values had to be discovered rather than created. Values had to be real and credible. They had to be embodied in the very fabric of the organization—in its systems processes, practices, and rewards, not just in its annual report or on wallet cards carried by the company's officers.

In order to create an impact of values the following must occur in an organization:

- People demonstrate and model the values in action in their personal work behaviors, decision-making, contribution and interpersonal interaction.
- Organizational values help each person establish priorities in their daily work life.
- Values guide every decision that is made once the organization has cooperatively created the values and the value statements.
- Rewards and recognition within the organization are structured to recognize those people whose work embodies the values the organization embraced.
- Organizational goals are grounded in the identified values.
- Adoption of the values and the behaviours that result is recognized in regular performance feedback
- People hire and promote individuals whose outlook and actions are congruent with the values.
- Only the active participation of all members of the organization will ensure a truly organization-wide, value-based, shared culture.

The employees who live by the values of the organizations show it by their efforts/purpose/direction/support by :

- Aligning all their actions/programs with the organization vision.
- Ailing all their actions/programs with the organization mission.
- Ailing all their actions/programs with the organization objectives.
- Ailing all their actions/programs with the organization strategies.
- In maximization of creation for customers
- In increasing value for company products for the market.

- In aligning company activities with the interest of shareholders.
- In managing risk in operation.
- In planning/budgeting.

The most visible characteristics that differentiate the companies are their values and the fact that the values come first, and acted as guiding principles that helped them to make crucial and difficult decisions. Values are inextricable from vision. For an organization to be well led, it needs a big idea to define its purpose. Its values must be clearly articulated—thus it states unambiguously what it stands for and guiding principles it will use in making decisions and governing its affairs. It may even be that it is more important for an organization to know what it stands for than where it is going, as the former will not change whereas the latter will change regularly in response to the issues of the day.

An effective and important leadership must perform the following functions:

- A leader should act as a friend, philosopher and guide to the people whom he is leading. He must have the capacity to recognize their potentialities and transform them in the realities.
- A leader should win the confidence of his people and seek their cooperation and convince them of policies, procedures and the goals to be achieved. He should be able to wipe out the differences among his people and unite them as a team and build up team spirit.
- He maintains discipline among his group and develops a sense of responsibility. He should be impartial in treating people under him and build up a high moral. He should as far as possible not use coercive methods. He should represent his people in and outside the organization. According to R. Likerts, "leaders act as linking pins between the work groups and the forces outside it."
- He should motivate his subordinates to achieve goals. He seeks their commitments to attain the objectives of the organization.

- He should try to raise high moral and ethical standards among his people.

To help leaders to develop the necessary leadership skills, training should be planned in four phase:

- Identify each leader's personal values. This requires individuals to consider when (in their career to date) they have been most satisfied, motivated, and valued at work. What values did this role satisfy? This enables the leader to enunciate perhaps for the first time, the values he or she inherently hold and often use as their basis for decision-making.
- Using their personal values as a base, leaders then develop a scenario of their ideal organization. Phase two requires managers, first as individuals and then in team, to describe their ideal organization. What does it look like? How does it function? What does it value?
- Leader's then assess their own organization against their ideal.

In phase three, managers compare their own organization to their ideal. What is inhibiting my organization from being more like my ideal? What enables my organization to be similar to my ideal? Compiling a list of inhibitors and enablers help managers see how personal values can relate to their organization's values.

- Leaders then develop strategies for moving both personally and organizationally towards the ideal.

The final phase involves developing strategies for translating the shared values into day-to-day actions. This must also include some personal and regular "walk the talk" type activities for every leader.

One of the most effective ways of doing this is to repeat the four-phase leadership training approach mentioned above with managers and staff throughout the organization and at every level. Each manager leads his/her team to assess the core values and how they can translate them into their field of operation.

Senior managers at the strategic level of the organization such as the heads of Marketing, Quality, HR, Finance, Production, IT, R&D, etc., should use this process to develop day-to-day action plans for translating values into action.

Organizations need leaders who can show the way and in whom people trust. Building leadership training on a solid foundation of corporate values can change the rhetoric into action so that leadership at all level becomes a case of "do as I do".

The core value of the organization bear the hallmark of the founder of the organization. They will have shaped and have been shaped by, the organizational processes, procedures and practices that are now part and parcel of the organizational life. And they will be revealed and reinforced by behaviours; traditions; rituals; and myth telling which have come to define 'the way we do things around here'.

Finally the determining factor in whether or not we can become a 'values-driven' business is how successful we are in translating our core values and those our workforce might not see as a core but are nevertheless important—into behavioural pattern that begins to transform performance. We may decide to do this by setting stretching performance targets or goals—we may decide to introduce self-improvement programmes or targets specific systems for change. Ultimately however we may never instill within our people a belief that 'continuous improvement' is good for them. But what we want is our people engaged in the business of improving about what they produce and how they produce and it can be achieved by behavioural change.

Resolving Value Conflict

S. Booma

In recent years organizational values has become a prominent issue. Most large organizations have a statement of corporate values and many organizations have programmes to promote these values among their employees and some financial organizations have taken steps of launching media advertising campaigns promoting not their product but their values. There is an emerging concept of values driven business and many organizations are thinking deeply about their standards of corporate behaviour and about the values that underpin the way they operate.

Today the corporate world is abandoning talk about business management and choosing instead to focus on corporate governance. Corporate leaders have started to realize the importance of values. There has been a major shift in perception also. Earlier there was a Darwinian concept of business: only the fittest survive; now it is tinged with a Confucian thought: only the virtuous thrive.

Values are the underlying dispositions that drive behaviour. At the macro organizational level the values embody an adaptive culture. These values are the core ideology, what they call 'a cult like culture'. This core ideology is made up of unchanged core purpose and are its core values.

Example:

SONY—has three core values—

1. Elevation of Japanese culture and national status.
2. Being a pioneer—not following others; doing the impossible.
3. Encouraging individual ability and creativity.

WALT DISNEY—Make People Happy

At the micro-level individuals too have their core values, ex: Honesty, excellence commitment, recognition, honesty and teamwork.

To what extent are organizational values the same as personal values? The congruence between the two is desirable and has important consequences. But they are not quit the same. Organizational values may be identical to personal values though they may be expressed in different terms. Some organizational values are in practice more like organizational goals or priorities (e.g. customer service). Nonetheless, if they are to be effective as a guide to individual behaviour, they should be related to and consistent with personal values held by individuals in the organization.

Why should there be an alignment of organizational values and personal values?

They should be a strong bridge between organizational and individual values. This link with value congruence is the fit with organization culture. People who don't fit either leave or are ejected.

The existence of shared values:

- Facilitates self-selection among potential employees.
- Can offer competitive advantage in a tight recruitment market.

- Mobilizes employee commitment.
- Offers a basis for the alignment of empowered staff members.
- Guides the organization's responses to crisis.

At the individual level value congruence is associated with—

- Feeling of personal success.
- Organizational commitment.
- Self-confidence and awareness in understanding personal and organizational values.
- Ethical behaviour.
- Feeling of stress (if there is low value congruence).
- The degree to which organizational goals were seen as important.
- The importance given to organizational stakeholders.

Many research papers have demonstrated a link between clarity of personal and organizational values and organizational commitment: the higher the level of clarity, the higher the level of commitment. People who are clearest about both sets of values had the highest level of commitment to organization.

For example, in the research paper by Peter Hyde and Bill Williamson. They have identified some top personal and organizational values. They are :

Top personal values	Top organizational values
Professionalism	Professionalism
Diligence	Honesty
Integrity	Integrity
Honesty	Staff well-being
Balance	Service to clients
Impartiality	Impartiality
Achievement	

The question is how do organizations select their values. Organization have to develop and promulgate core values in the same way that mission statements and strategies are developed. These core values have to be distilled and they cannot be created but must be discovered. Organizations cannot select as their values what the outside world thinks should be their values rather the key to good selection lies in choosing what is authentically believed in. Only then will there be a congruence of organizational and individual values. Such alignment will help achieve business objectives.

- Promote behaviour associated with core values.
- Remove processes that conflict with core values.

If there are misalignment of values the values should not be discarded. Nor should the organization adopt new market driven value statements in which they do not completely believe in. Rather it would be worth exploring the context of misalignment and to try and describe the values in different terms—terms that help to connect.

This is best illustrated by the story related by Sir Adrian Cadbury, former chairman of Cadbury Schweppes PLC and best known for the formulation of the Cadbury Code, a code of best practices which has served as a basis and inspiration for corporate governance reforms around the world. It also reveals that there is no simple, universal formula to deal with ethical problems.

We will have to choose from our own codes of conduct what rules to apply to case in hand; the outcome of those choices defines who we are:

> "In 1900, Queen Victoria sent a decorative tin with a bar of chocolate inside to all her soldiers who were serving South Africa. These tins still turn up today, often complete with their contents, a tribute to the collecting instinct. At the time, the order faced my grandfather with an ethical dilemma. He owned and ran the second largest chocolate factory in Britain, so he was trying harder and the order meant additional work for the factory. Yet he was deeply and publicly apposed to the Anglo-Boer war. He resolved the dilemma by accepting the order, but carrying out at cost. He therefore made no profit out of what he saw as an unjust war, his employees benefited from the additional work the soldier received their royal present and I am will

sent the tins", said Sir Adrian. "My grandfather was able to resolve the conflict between the decision best for the business and his personal code of ethics because he and his family owned the firm which bore their name".

Resolving Conflicts

Only men of wisdom know to resolve such a value dilemma. Alignment of values or value congruence can be brought about only when we kindle the human energies. There are four kind of human energies—physical, intellectual, emotional and spiritual. We have to tap on the EQ and SQ to align our values.

The importance of vision and values, to align personal goals with those of the organization was highlighted in the cover story of *Business Week*. Newly appointed CEO (Barrett) at Intel is tasked with turning around a business that is in trouble but with a long track record of success. The success was delivered through a focus on a single vision "Intel inside" and clarity of insight into the role and impact of technology.

Recent changes in strategy led to Intel playing the role of venture capitalist and diversifying outside its core business of designing and making micro-chips. However, Barrett says, "His strategy has not created a company without focus".

Here is a good example of a "blue-chip" company where the business leader is attempting to take the organization into new directions to sustain its growth. His personal vision and values are, for the moment, at odds with the market and indeed the ability of the organization as a whole to align behind his vision and values. This is just a single illustration of a situation that plays out on a daily basis for business leaders in almost all organizations.

How then does one motive people (the organization) to align with the theory of the business? According to Herzberg (1968) one does not use the carrot or the stick because in both cases the people are moving to the leader's motives. Instead one has to work towards getting people to want to move towards the common vision. In organizations this implies a major role for the leader to build an environment in which people will want to align with the vision and values. Consider the definition of a team as "a small number of people with complementary skills who are committed to a common purpose, set of performance goals and approach for which they hold themselves mutually accountable" (Katzenbach and Smith, 1998).

Securing the motivation of people who write academic and research papers carried out more out of a personal gain through publications rather than to serve society. They are concerned with personal motivation rather than with a fit with the organization's common set of ideas or core ideologies.

Values and Spirituality

Values of individuals and organizations need to be in harmony if people are to 'want' to move towards a vision. A question that arises now is whether alignment of personal and organizational goal leads to spirituality or whether the journey to the inner-self leads to alignment. This is a complex question. To quote Ken Blanchard, 'We are not human beings having a spiritual experience. We are spiritual beings having a human experience'. If we could tackle all value conflicts with a sense of duty and sacrifice we would be able to resolve conflicting situations in organizations. Using a spiritual quotient to resolve conflicts will bring about some alignment but all conflicting values cannot be aligned. We should not disregard these rather it would be appropriate to describe these values in different terms—into behavioural patterns that help to transform performance.

Success in any organization is about the utilization of human energy. The only way to tap this energy is to make people your partner. The only way to do this is to create some meaning in their activities and show concern for them. Preserve the core, stimulate progress.

Importance of Corporate Culture in Merger Processes

S. Kayalvizhi

A true merger occurs when both businesses dissolve and fold their assets and liabilities into a newly created entity. Acquisition is taking possession of another business, also called a takeover or buyout.

According to an ATK earney research study, it is a problem in many mergers that the more powerful partner imposes his culture on the less powerful one. This is done without any evaluation which culture would be the more suitable one for the new organization. This approach may lead to a successful merger and integration quickly in some situations. In other situations, however, this approach will destroy much of the value that was expected to grow from the merger. Especially when both partners are very different, it needs a closer evaluation, which culture will be best for both together.

A perfect integration (which is rarely achieved in practice) would develop a new culture from both former cultures of the partners. Ideally, this new culture should include the best elements from both organizations. Reality often looks different. Cultural pluralism and cultural blending do not work in cases. The results are cultural resistance followed by a cultural takeover. The problem in mergers is that people from very different organizations (and cultures) are expected to work together, to discuss, and to solve complex strategic and operative tasks. It is very difficult to impose a new culture that does not have the acceptance of the people.

Difference in work culture was a major mismatch in case of TCL's acquisition of Alcatel as motivation incentives which worked in China had no effect on the French. In fact, long work hours and bonuses based on the time employees put in was something that the French just did not understand since they came from different economic situations. Not only did this slow down TAMP's progress, it put many issues on the backburner which could only end up affecting one thing: the company's bottom-line.

In September 2005, Munich-based BenQ, an Asian telecommunication and electronics major, acquired the mobile phone division of Siemens. But, did not even last a full year in the green and was soon followed by a bankruptcy filing, Why did this happen? With so many synergies in place, what went wrong? It took BenQ Mobile less than a year to bid farewell to the six thousand employees they inherited from Siemens Mobile.

INTERNATIONALIZATION OF INDIAN COMPANIES

The giant positive strides that Brand India has taken in last few years is nothing less than astonishing. Indian Businessmen and Entrepreneurs are set out to revamp Indian image that will be boasting world's biggest corporations in near future. All the sectors, be it Steel, manufacturing, Information technology, Auto and FMCG are all buzzing with Mega Indian acquisitions. The latest and probably the most talked about after Mittal's buy out of Arcelor, is Jaguar—Land Rover bid by Tata group. Ford Motor Co. sold Jaguar Land Rover to Tata Motors Ltd. for $2.3 billion, for almost half the price it paid while acquiring them.

The outsourcing phenomenon, especially in IT Industry has helped Indian companies in lot of direct and indirect ways. First and foremost, it has ensured that Indian managers and executives are now far more exposed to western business culture and practices. Over a period of time, the Indian offshore companies have created an image of reliable low cost, yet high quality products and services. Outsourcing offshoring companies have increased their profits exponentially. There is a lot more cash available with Indian companies than ever before. Their capacity to borrow large amount of cash has also gone high.

POST M&A PROBLEMS

Preoccupation

In Canada, individual preoccupation with "How is this all going to impact me?" weakens commitment to the job at hand. This, in turn, translates into people looking for work in other companies. Often a firm in the midst of transition loses some of its own talent—strengthening the competition. In countries where people identify largely with groups, people tend to look for support within their group. In France and Italy, people caught in the midst of a merger or acquisition often turn to unions. If unions cannot provide answers because they have been excluded from the negotiation process, they are likely to go on strike. These strikes may do much more damage to the organization that comparable Canadian strikes: for example, the strike by French railroad and subway workers in December 1995 resulted in the demise of the Juppe government, what is less apparent is the pervasive loss of productivity of those who remain. Studies indicate that line employees and managers at all levels lose a minimum of 15% of personal effectiveness as a result of rumors and misinformation. They also indicate that teams tend to break down and become less effective during mergers and acquisitions.

INFREQUENT AND IRRELEVANT COMMUNICATION

In many international M&As, the working languages of the two organizations involved are not the same. Communication can break down even when the employees of the foreign M&A target speak English. Consider the case of a Norwegian-American joint venture. Because Norwegians tend to be more relationship-oriented while Americans tend to focus on tasks, the parties almost came to blows over when and how to bring the discussions to a conclusion. The Norwegians complained that they had not built up enough trust to negotiate final details and needed more time. The Americans responded that they could not waste valuable time on further meetings and that the matter should be settled by the legal team. Tension decreased when the teams realized that their goals were the same but their ways of achieving them were quite different: a deal was eventually struck.

Triangulation

Without clear lines of authority and clear understanding of where they fit in, employees and managers are caught in a web of conflating objectives and old loyalties. This type of organizational and personal strangulation robs the new entity of the very energy kit needs to oversome the losses in productivity. The tolerance for "fuzzy", temporary organizational charts and decision-making processes depend on the countries involved in the merger or acquisition. In hierarchical countries, like the Philippines, both organizational chart and chain of command need to be clearly defined, more clearly than in Canada. If employees do not understand them, paralysis often results. A Filipino employee reporting to two managers, as in a matrix organization will likely be quickly overwhelmed. He/She interpret the situation as having to meet two complete sets of expectations and performs two separate jobs. For Filipinos, asking managers to discuss their conflicting requests would be viewed as insubordination.

PEOPLE ISSUES AS A MAJOR DRIVER OF M&A UNDERPERFORMANCE

Cultural-due-diligence looks at corporate cultures and attempts to ascertain an organizational fit between the two merging companies. Each company will have its own culture, derived from several components—corporate policies, rules, compensation plans, leadership styles, internal communication, physical work environment, etc. Cultural-due-diligence attempts to answer the question to what extent can the two companies change and adapt to differences between the two corporate cultures. The wider the cultural gap, the more difficult it will be to integrate the two companies.

It is very important to get the Human Resource Department involved in the Merger and Acquisition process, since they have strong insights into cultural and human resource issues. [(Coopers (2001)] Failure to tackle the people issues such as retaining top talent and communication effectively with the work force is one of the reasons why the majority of deals fail to meet expectations.

Since the opening of the Indian economy in 1991, Tata has been subject to global competition, making it imperative for the group to become competitive in India against the new entrants. To gain scale, reduce their exposure to the cyclicality of India's economy, survive, and achieve a sustainable competitive position in industries that are globalizing, most Tata companies then looked overseas. Tata's recent experience is an excellent case for analyzing 'accelerated internationalization'. As it pertains to a challenger conglomerate from formerly peripheral areas that goes international in order to access resources, the Tata group has been driven by multiple factors, including the need to access new markets (e.g., in BPO services), the opportunity to integrate the value chain (e.g., in steel), and the quest for brand control (e.g., in tea). This strategy proved feasible because. Tata possesses strong leadership combined with vision: can exploit the possibility of leveraging increasingly developed financial markets in India, a large domestic market, and global liquidity: and reacted fast to the opening of specific opportunities at given times.

PART IV

Organizational Life : A Holistic View

Spiritual Values in Organizational Life : An Invigorating Force to Reckonwith to Attain Corporate Success

M. ANBALAGAN AND V. GUGARAMAN

With the advent of globalization, the evils of other civilizations are haunting us, especially in corporate world. With constraint on time and relaxation being sought thro' petty means, the present working world is witnessing moral degeneration, disharmony in family and depression. Corporate employees expect and need meaningful existence and the corporate leadership is looking for new ways to motivate employees and create innovative solutions for corporate challenges. What is the answer? The answer is "Spirituality".

(i) Can spiritually bring edge?

(ii) Is it possible to maximize ethics and profits together in business?

(iii) How to eliminate stress associated with the modern lifestyle and promote well-being at physical, mental and spiritual level?

(iv) According to Napoleon Bonaparte, there are only two powers in the world—the spirit and sword. In the long-run sword will always be defeated by the spirit.

(v) Great warriors like Alexander had a lot of weapons either to establish or defend himself. But there was a saint who had nothing. His illuminated words, thought and deeds conquered every great thing. This weaponless saint is called "Mahaveer".

(vi) Spirituality offers us a methodology to deepen our awareness of our inner being and from this develop or change the 'self' in the ways that are conductive to the kind of corporate culture we want.

(vii) Spiritual values are 'Universal' and pertain to pure consciousness and harnessing of inner potential.

Power of Spiritual Values in Corporate Success

The term "spirituality" is derived from the Latin Word 'Spiritus', which means vapour breath, air or wind. The Tamil word of Spirituality "Aan megam" (Aanma-soul) is more apt and suitable.

The values of truth, righteousness, peace, love and violence are found in all major spiritual paths. These spiritual values are also human values and are the fundamental roots for a healthy, vibrant and viable work career.

"Spiritual values" are something that human beings need to aspire and hopefully something to achieve. We know that most people see 'human nature' as nothing but spiritual—they typically see it as limited, imperfect, and so on. However, we know that we are "spiritual being" first, and that "to be human is to be spiritual". So by calling these spiritual values "human values", it reminds us that they are inherent in our spiritual nature.

Business houses may not wrong to mention that exercise their power based on spiritual values generate more sustainable corporate success and more global economic prosperity.

What is the source of this energy? Now, this is an ageless and endless inquiry into the very origin of creation. And that brings us to the arena of spirituality.

We hesitate, perhaps for good reason, to bring to integrate the subjects of spirituality and business. Some people fear for the "corporate takeover" of our values and souls. Some fear that conflicts over differences in beliefs could disrupt corporate life inappropriately. Even so, corporate success in these changing times is a challenging journey that demands new means for navigating difficult roads (including the information highways). The curves are sharper, and the road goes through a very stormy terrain. And that's what business power is about; an energized, vital set of people working together to manifest and achieve something significant! So the question of, "how do we bring business into our sense or spirituality?" is potentially the most stimulating, far-reaching, and path breaking question for business people to discover the nature of business power.

The great spiritual literature documents nine key principles that make up the foundation walls, and roof of our spiritual home. Within this context of spiritual power. We can attempt to find a room for a new understanding of the nature of business power.

1. There is a single God, who is the omnipotent source of manifesting and vitalizing this creation.
2. There is a more permanent "reality" than the temporary phenomena of this "material" world.
3. There is an entity—that exists separate from and beyond the death of the body.
4. Man's soul shares in the divine nature of God, as created in God's image.
5. The goal of life is to realize and experience this union with God, primarily through selfless love.
6. This union with God includes a sense of oneness with all people and creation, through love.
7. This sense of love and oneness naturally expresses itself actively, as service to others.
8. The purpose of having a body is to have an instrument (a means) for realizing union with God and for serving others.
9. The evidence of spiritual growth is congruence of thought, word and deed in expressing basic spiritual values.

Five basic values—love, truth, responsible action, inner peace, and non-violence—are found in all spiritual foundations. For example, we find the Dukkappttadigatha saying, "Give charity (right action) out of devotion (love), always maintain the moral precepts (truth and non-violence), find delight in mediation (inner peace), and you will attain the celestial life".

This spiritual view says that evidence of spiritual growth in congruence of thought, word, and deed is found in the expression of core spiritual/human values. As mentioned earlier, five core values—love, truth, responsible action, inner peace, and non-violence directly support business success. For example:

Truthfulness—foster trust and honest communications.
Responsible action—fosters high quality work.
Inners peace—fosters creative and wise decisions.
Love—fosters great service based on caring for other's well being.
Non-violence—fosters win-win collaboration.

These five values are found in all spiritual traditions. Therefore, Spiritual Values are the fundamental underpinnings to sustainable business success.

We can consider the case of AT & T consumer Products, handling their residential telephone business with 13,000 people. In 1985, it had been the least profitable division of AT & T, and the job of turning it around was given to Senior VP and Chief Quality Officer Ken Bertaccini. He was also given an ultimantum: turn it around in two years, or the business world be abandoned. One of the initiatives he sponsored was a training program focused on living and working with much greater levels if honesty, integrity, commitment, and caring—it was called "Project Miracles", run by Harvin Rutigliano. As a result within the two year time frame, this division become one of the most profitable in AT & T and had the highest morale as well.

HOW SPIRITUAL VALUES WORK?

Peak-performing organisations demand a mastery of their

own collective power to create. Our original sources for this comes from our relationship to creation itself; since we are integral parts of creation, and as such, share its creative power. We can focus the power of create ideas for two purposes in business; to achieve greater revenues (for the "top line" on a balance sheet) and to achieve greater efficiency of work processes (affecting the "midline" areas of the balance sheet). In addition, innovation can be either evolutionary. Truth telling, love, business—they need each other. Spiritual values such as truth and love enrich business success.

Not all companies operating by spiritual values will necessarily succeed—it takes business acumen and skill as well. What they all will do is to embody the spirit that when we serve, we can be serving God and advancing our spiritual wisdom. It allows us our work as a spiritual fulfilment of the mystics' vision for life. As Christ and others have stated, when we serve even the least of our brethren, we are doing it also directly to and for God". This allows us to "Love God and Serve God" simultaneously as we "Love all and Serve all". Then the between worship and come quickly rumbling down.

It's too late to argue about whether spirituality belongs in the work place or doesn't. Our souls go to work with us, and it's time to express our spirituality consciously. We have to stop working six days and worshipping separately for an hour on the seventh day.

If you choose to make it your personal, you could bring the power of your spiritual values to your won work place. Here's one starting point. Perhaps you'll think of others as well.

1. *Truthfulness*: speak honestly with employees and customers; speak directly rather than behind someone's back, speak unarguably in terms of facts rather than opinions.
2. *Responsible Action*: conduct business with fair prices and ethical practices; keep your agreements, with employees as well as customers; take responsibility for problems, rather than making excuses.
3. *Inner Peace*: practice equanimity, even in crises, in times of profit or loss, and in times of praise or blame; see

yourself as the source of your emotional reactions, rather than the victim of someone else's behaviour.

4. *Love*: connect to a higher purpose in your life in which you can care for and serve others through your work; listen generously and compassionately to others rather than beings judgmental.
5. *Non-Violence*: conduct business that is environmentally friendly; find win-win solutions to problems, rather than winning at another's expense.

These values are "build in" to our human nature; they do not have to be inculcated, just evoked. What would these look like around you? It means a clerical person would do his or her best quality work, even if no one was watching. It means a professional would tell about the errors or delays, even if it mean a temporary reprimand. It means an executive would continually strive to find creative new ways to deliver goods faster, without costly delays to his or her customers. It means a sales person would not over-promise what a product would do or overcharge for them. It means a manager would actively seek to resolve a customer complaint rather than hide behind bureaucratic rules.

LIVING UP TO THE POTENTIAL AND RESPONSIBILITY

Truly, spiritual values such as love, truth, peace, right action and non-violence usher in a new golden era in business activities. The world at large the spirit within each of us, calls upon us to recognize our inherent spiritual nature and to bring it in to our work. Pure consciousness is pure potentiality; it is the field of all possibilities and infinite creativity. Pure consciousness is our spiritual essence. Being, infinite and unbounded, it is also pure joy. Other attributes of consciousness are pure knowledge, infinite silence, perfect balance, invincibility, simplicity and bliss. This is our essential nature. Our essential nature is one of pure potentiality. When the mission of the business is to serve, it taps into the most profound and noble, levels of the human spirit. In the spiritual context, responsibility means not blaming anyone or anything for your situation, including yourself. Having accepted this circumstance, this event, this problem, responsibility then means the ability to have a creative response to the situation as it is now. All problems contain the seeds of opportunity and this awareness allows one to take the moment and transform it to a better situation or thing. Once we do this, every so-called upsetting situation will become an opportunity for the creation of something new and beautiful, and every so-called tormentor or tyrant will become our teacher. Reality is an interpretation. And if we choose to interpret reality in this way, we will have many teachers around us, and many opportunities to evolve.

Business has to play a key role in transforming our society and our quality of life. Certainly the problems of the world in this millennium demand our deepest, most sincere effort to "clean up our mess". But even more, our souls urge us to ignite our lives with spiritual purpose, and rededicate out work to making a difference, not must making money, to be concerned with good not just goods.

Willis Harman, in Global Mind Change, points out what the opportunities and the responsibilities that business leaders (at all levels!) face as we approach the early days of the 21st Century.

Leader in world business are first expected to be the true planetary citizens. They have worldwide capability and responsibility; their domains transcend national boundaries. Their decisions affect not just economies, but societies; and not just direct concerns of business, but world problems such as poverty, environment and security.

Effective Organizational Culture and Divine Guidance

M. AKBAR MOHIDEEN

The possibility of an organization to achieve success in a dynamic setting is not determined just by the strategy-structure and the reward system that make up its visible features. Rather, every organization has an invincible quality, a certain style, a character, and a way of doing things that ultimately determines whether success will be achieved. That is what we call 'culture' of the organization. Once an individual joins an organization, he or she will imbibe, or be specialized into, the culture that is specific to that organization. Organization Culture can be defined as "the shared values, norms, behaviour patterns, rituals and traditions in an organization". It is more powerful than the dictates of any one person or any formally documented system. To understand the soul of an organization, therefore, requires a discussion of Cultural Values. It is the common knowledge that the cultural values propounded by the Creator (Almighty God) are more effective. The divine knowledge revealed in the Holy Quran and the life of the final Prophet, Mohamed (peace be upon him) and his rightly guided companions are the bedrock of the Islamic culture. An organization will be the most successful one when this culture is practiced.

ISLAMIC CULTURE AND ITS VALUE STRUCTURE

Islam is an Arabic word. It is derived from two root-words: One *Salm,* meaning peace and the other *Silm* meaning submission. Islam stands for "a commitment to surrender one's will to the Will of God" and thus to be at peace with the Creator and with all that has been created by Him. Religion and secularism are not two autonomous categories; they represent two sides of the same coin.

The following concepts generate the basic values of an Islamic Culture.

1. Belief in one God (*Tawhid*)

The essential comprehensive characteristic of Islam and its primary basis is the unity of God, which affirms the radical monotheism of Islam. God is One, He has no partner and there is none worthy of worship except him. This belief extends to all of creation and thus signifies unity of God, the unity of the community of the faithful, the unity of life as a totality, and the unity of the temporal and spiritual. This provides one, single direction and guarantees a unified spirit for its adherents. It perfects the ethical consciousness of mankind and enters humanity with the hidden power of "wisdom", which nurtures and perfects it.

The belief in one God Who is the Most Powerful and who is the Sustainer of this Universe, freed the Companions of Prophet of any fear from anything other than their Lord. It gave them a sense of confidence that made them more generous and more courageous. It is applicable to all believers.

2. Belief in the hereafter and Reward and Punishment

The culture of the Companions of the prophet is also characterised by the belief in the Hereafter during which they will face reward in paradise or punishment in Hell. This firm belief in Hereafter and in reward and punishment created an attitude of self-control among the Companions. Indeed they were feeling accountable for every tiny action they took. The Hereafter comprised the long-term objective of the Companion who strived hard to enter Paradise and to avoid Hell. This means that the belief in the Hereafter represented a great measure for motivating the Companion of the Prophet to do righteous deeds and to avoid any wrong doings. The belief in the Oneness of God and the Hereafter entails the belief in the unity of the creation and destiny of mankind. In fact, the pillars of the Islamic faith include the belief in other revelations and Prophet such as Abraham, Moses, and Jesus (May Allah's Peace be upon them all). This is evident in the following verse of the Quran: "*Say Ye, We believe in Allah and the revelations given to us and Abraham, Ismaeel, Isaac, Jacob and the tribes and that given to Moses and Jesus and that given to (all) prophets from their Lord. We make no difference between one and another of them and We (bow and) submit to Allah*". (Quran 2:136).

3. Vicegerency *(Khilafah)*

A corollary of *tawhid* is *khilafah, i.e.* mankind is vicegerent of God. As a vicegerent, mankind is not free but responsible and accountable to Allah. One's vocation and destiny, therefore, is the service of Allah, or fulfilment of Divine Will. Allah has "*not created Mankind and Jinn but to serve him.*" (Quran 51:56) The *khilafah* consists of the fulfilment of the responsibility under two headings: The first one is, duties and obligations due directly to God, and the second is, duties to oneself, to fellow beings and to other creatures for the pleasure of God in accordance with the will of God. The faithful execution of this sublime responsibility is, in fact, the true nature of worship or service to God.

4. Worship *(Ibadah)*

The concept of worship is very wide in Islam. It does not mean merely ritual or specific form of prayer, but a life of continuous prayer and unremitting obedience to Allah. Worship encompasses all activities of life—spiritual, social, economic, and political—provided they are in accordance with the rules as laid down and if their ultimate objective is to seek the pleasure of God. Worshipping God means, all actions we undertake should be for the sake of God. Whatever we do with the intention of pleasing God is considered worship. Focusing our life on this single purpose makes us very efficient. All our actions and intentions become so coherent. Having more than one supreme goal will tear our capabilities apart and ultimately impede our success.

5. Knowledge *(Ilm)*

Among the many manifestations of worship and a pre-requisite to its effective performance is knowledge. In its totality the concept of knowledge in Islam is very vast. Knowledge, in general, is divided into two categories: revealed knowledge, which basically includes the *Quran* and the *Sunnah,* and science-derived knowledge, which is acquired through experience, observation and research.

Knowledge is mentioned in the Quran with unusual frequency and has been paired, in verse 30:56, with faith, which, according to verse 3:71, follows upon truth. The pursuit of knowledge, according to a Hadith, is incumbent upon every Muslim even if it entails traveling far off China. However, knowledge becomes a value only if it is pursued within the value-framework of Islam. Unlike the Western hackneyed phrase of "knowledge for knowledge sake" or that entire convoluted argument that "all knowledge is good," Islam considers knowledge as a value and an act of worship only when it is pursued for the benefit of the individual or humanity and ultimately for gaining the pleasure of God.

6. Responsibility and Accountability

Responsibility and accountability are attributes that are very important in determining self-control and honesty. These two important attributes stem from the belief in the Hereafter and in reward and punishment. The Prophet (pbuh) said.

Behold! Each one of you is guardian and each one of you will be asked about his subjects. A leader is a guardian over the people and he will be asked about his subjects. A man is guardian over the members of his household and he will be asked about his subjects; a woman is guardian over the members of the household of the husband and of his children. Behold! Each one of you is a guardian and each one of you will be asked about his subjects." —(Bukhari)

Changes should come from within first and thus the Muslims should always strive to change themselves and their environment for the better. They should not wait of others such as their leaders or supervisors to make the change. Leaders should also not blame their followers for their failures. They should always blame themselves, review their intentions and strive for the better.

7. Participation and Consultation

The culture of the companion of the prophet was a culture of participation through consultation, advice and forbidding the wrong and. enjoining good. Consultations are mandatory in Islam, and more importantly, it displayed a way of life. The climate of participation that resigned during the time of the Companions was very fertile for innovation, satisfaction, participation, efficiency, and adaptiveness.

Participation take the form of *Shura* (consultation) in order to make better decision, correcting the wrong in order to reduce defects and advice in order to improve performance. Consultation is an exercise aimed at reaching a consensus. If the consensus is not reached then people have to stick to the majority. Prophet Mohamed (pbuh) also said, *"My nation cannot agree upon an error and if a conflict persists be with the majority".* —(Ibnu Majah)

Commenting on the weakness of a single opinion and the strength of multiple opinions, "Caliph Omar made the analogy between a single opinion and a single string of thread, and multiple opinions and a strong rope.

8. Justice and Equity

The cornerstone of the culture of the Companions was justice, one of the major goals of Islam. In the Holy Quran, *"Allah commands justice, benevolence, and liberality to kith and kin, and He forbids all shameful deeds, and injustice and transgression; He instructs you, that yet may receive admonition".* —(Quran16: 90)

Justice and compassion are two other essential characteristics a leader must possess. Justice without compassion leads to tyranny, while compassion without justice creates anarchy. Justice demands that all subordinates should be given equal opportunity according to their abilities. A leader needs to maintain a careful balance keeping the overall good of his followers in mind, justly and fairly regardless of their race, colour, origin, or religion. The Quran commands Muslims to be fair even when dealing with those opposed to them.

"O you who believe! Stand out firmly for God as witnesses to fair dealing and let not the hatred of others to you make you swerve to wrong and depart from justice, Be just; that is next to piety".

—(Quran 5:8)

"Allah does command you to render back your trusts to those to whom they are due and when you judge between people that you judge with justice". —(Quran 4:58

"O you who believe! Stand out firmly for justice, as witness. To Allah, even as against yourselves or your parents, or your kin, and whether it be (against) rich or poor". —(Quran 4:135)

Like a true leader of men, Caliph Omar (Ral) inflicted on his own son who was found guilty of drunkenness, eighty stripes, according to the prevailing law. The son could not survive the full rigor of the punishment but the dignity of justice, equity and good conscience, which the commander of the faithful had upheld, has made his leadership an unforgettable lesson for the world.

9. Trust, Dignity and Privacy

Islam emphasises the dignity of mankind irrespective of their race, gender or religion. Allah, the Exalted said: *"We have honoured the children of Adam, provided them with transport on the land and the sea, given them for sustenance things good and pure and conferred on them special favours above a great part of Our Creation".*

—(Quran 17:70).

Recognising the dignity of people means respecting them and respecting their privacy. Indeed, Islam places important emphasis on the privacy of man. This is evident in the Prophet's teaching that if one visits another, he must knock thrice at his host door and if he did not receive any permission to enter, he must leave. With regard to dignity, it is one of the basic elements of life that must be safeguarded.

People who don't trust one another might resort to spying and counter-spying something—which leads to the waste of time, efforts and mental focus. Trust prevailed in the relationships between the Companions. Mutual trust existed between the leaders and their followers, and among the followers. The openness and directness of the Companions supported this trust. Prophet Mohamed (pbuh) also said: *"A leader who is suspicious of his people will lead them to mischief."*

—(Abu Dawood)

10. Cost and Time Efficiency

The Companions were taught by the Prophet about cost efficiency to such an extent that they should use the minimum amount of water necessary while doing their ablution even if the water is in abundant. Islam discourages spending for luxury rather encourages moderate spending for ones comfort. Extravagance is strongly condemned. Allah, the Exalted, says: *"O Children of Adam! eat and drink but waste not by 'extravagance'. Certainly He (Allah) likes not who waste by 'extravagance."*

—(Quran 7:31)

"Verily, spendthrifts are brothers of Satan and the Satan is ever ungrateful to his Lord". —(Quran 17:26)

While time means money in the West, it means 'Life" in Islam. Whatever we lose is lost from our limited life for which we are accountable. The Prophet (pbuh) said: *"Man will be asked about his life, how he spent it, his youth, how he used it and his money, how he earned it and how he spent it."* —(Tirmidhi)

Regarding time efficiency and about spending the time in this world in pleasing the Almighty Allah in all walks of life, The Prophet (bpuh) said: *"Take advantage of five before five: your youth before your aging, your health before your sickness, your wealth before your poverty, your free time before your busy time, and your life before your death."* —(Tirmidhi)

11. Caring and sharing

Caring is necessary for the success of any organization. Be it a family or an MNC. We shall care about our clients, subordinates and colleagues. Caring leads to helping and sharing. When we help our colleagues when they are going through some difficulties, we are actually helping the organization by getting the job well done and by promoting a culture of mutual support.

The culture of the Companions was also a culture of caring and sharing. It was a culture of mercy towards fellow human beings as well as with the animals and nature. Islam established a real sense of collectiveness and community among companions the Prophet who felt like one body that feels the pain whenever one of its members suffers. Prophet Mohamed (pbuh) said: *"The believers are like one man, if his head is in pain his whole body suffers and if his eye is in pain his whole body suffers."* —(Bukhari)

12. Mercy Towards Humans, Animals and the Environment

Islam also requires its followers to be merciful towards everything on this earth. Prophet Mohamed (pbuh) said:*"Be Merciful with those on the earth, you have the Mercy of the One Who is in the heaven (Allah)."* —(Tirmidhi)

Islam values the creatures of God, which includes besides the honoured human being, the animals and the environment. As for animals, Prophet Mohamed (pbuh) said: *"A woman will be punished in Hell-Fire because she confined a cat. She neither fed it, nor did she allow it to roam on the land in search of food."* —(Muslim)

When asked whether helping an animal is rewarded in Islam Prophet Mohamed (pbuh) replied: *"There is reward in helping every living soul."* —(Ibnu Majah)

Muslims have been prohibited from cutting trees, polluting wells, and burning books during the time of war (in protecting both the environment and civilization of even the enemies). The care that Muslims have to show toward the creatures, stems from the belief that every thing belongs to God and that humans are the vicegerents of God in the universe. This means that people have the right to use the environment but they have no right to abuse it.

The research findings of many successful organizations in India and abroad reveal that the strong culture with the above mentioned value structure makes them outperform their competitors and retain their lead position. More importantly, the leadership of an organization influence organizational culture. Leaders should realize that they are the role models and that their behaviour is reflected on the culture of their organization. The leader's strong positive culture through words and actions inspire employees to deliver better and this success is sustained for a long period. Such cultural values, ethical aspects and moral standards should be inculcated among the employees through a systematic action plan.

24

Enriching Managerial and Personal Life in Islamic Culture

S. SHAMSUDDIN

In today's dynamic business world, it has become extremely important for companies to constantly change according to the situation, restructure their business module and revamp their products. In this scenario a few companies survive and successful and others fall or disappear altogether. What are the qualities or values that make some companies more successful than others and retain their lead position? To answer this question, the researcher has found the culture of the organization.

Just as people may choose to move to a certain geographic region on the basis of its characteristics such as temperature, humidity and rainfall, employees also gravitate towards the organizational culture they prefer as a work environment. Most cultures evolve directly from the examples s bytop management, who have a powerful influence on their employees.

Research evidence indicates that there is a positive relationship between certain organizational culture and performance. In a survey of over 43,000 employees in 34 companies, one researcher concluded, "The cultural and behavioural characteristics of organization have a measurable effect on a company's performance. One such is Islamic culture.

ISLAMIC CULTURE

Islamic culture is based on Quran and Hadeeth, which are divine sources. The Glorious book is the Book of Allah, the wise and worthy of all praise, who has promised to safeguard it from any violations in its purity. Praise to be Allah the cherisher and sustainer of the words, who has said in this noble book.

"These has come to you from Allah
Light and perspicuous Book".

—(Q 5:15)

The Arabic work 'Hadeeth' refers to the literature, which consists of the narrations of the life of the prophet (SAW) and the things approved by him. It covers the narrations about the companies and successors as well.

"Mankind is a fold every member of which shall
be a keeper or shephered unto every other, and
be accountable for the welfare of the entire fold".

—Bukhari

In Islamic Culture, an organization is a family of God. In it, an employer, manager, supervisor, employee and others are the members of a family. They are all brothers and sisters. They should love and be affectionate with each other for the pleasure of God. They should help each other. The vision of the organization and manager is to get pleasure of God.

ENRICHING MANAGERIAL AND PERSONAL LIFE

The word 'Enrich' means improving quality or values. Managerial life refers to work life of managers. Quality is everyone's responsibility in any organization. Quality demands that one should perform the best. It gives importance to people issues rather than the technical issues performing quality work is an accountability of manager, employee, worker, etc. The word 'manager' means man and manager, it includes both personal and organizational. A large number of managers in the West and Japan have been practicing various qualities to improve their personal and organizational life. James, a manager writes that "No battle for maker share has yet been won by a formula or a computer—they have been won in the final analysis by hard fighting and by practical hands on experience of an executive who is able to make intuitively right decision at the right place at the right time.

Several thinkers in the field of management claim today it is not the politicians, social workers, or swamis but the managers who are the real change agents in the organization. Most of the western paradigms whether capitalist or Marxist are giving importance to material world of managers in order to retain them. Even then, they are leaving the organization. Therefore, there is search for alternative paradigm i.e., Divine guidance.

The following are the Islamic qualities which will enrich the managerial life and personal life.

(1) *Sincerity*: Sincerity is one of the qualities required for improving managerial and personal life. Sincerity is the freeing of one's intentions from all impurities in order to come nearer to God. It is to ensure that the intention behind all acts and deeds in personal and managerial life are exclusively for His pleasure.

> *"And they have commanded to worship*
> *only Allah, being sincere towards*
> *Him in their deen and true".*
>
> —(Q 98:5)

(2) *Patience*: One of the qualities for reliving stress in personal life and work life is patience. Islam asked the people to be stead fast, patience and to help one another, maintain patience while doing the righteous

work. They should satisfy the God to get His pleasure.

"Patiently them pressure, for the
promise of Allah is true......"

—(Q. 40:55)

(3) *Forgiveness*: One of the qualities for resolving conflict in life and work life is forgiveness. The manager for the sake of the pleasure of God should forgive the mistake committed by family member and sub-ordinates, colleagues in his organization.

*"Who master their anger, and forgive other
God loveth the doers of good".*

—(Q. 3:133)

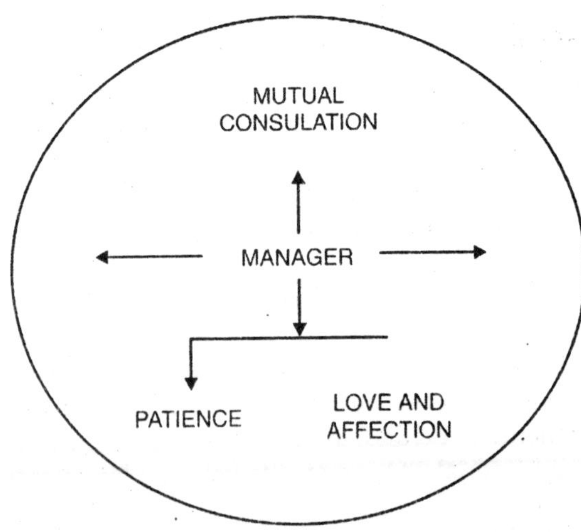

(4) *Mutual consultation*: One of the qualities for resolving the conflict in life and work life is mutual consultation. It is a mutual consultation among the family members or employees to discuss the problem and take a decision for the pleasure of God. The Quran has made it clear that leaders (Managers) obligated to consult those who have knowledge or those who can provide sound advice.

"More enduring is a portion with God
whose affairs are guided by mutual counsel".

—(Q. 42:30)

(5) *Love and Affection*: One of the qualities for improving personal life and work life in an organization is love and affection. The manager should have love and affection towards his family members and employers for the pleasure of God. This reduces stress and conflict is an organization.

"The believing men and believing women
are protecting friends of one another".

—(Q. 9:71)

If you love some one, you should express your love to that person. Its psychological affect on that person will be that he will develop a sense of nearness to you. Love will no longer be merely a feeling confined within heart but will begin to play a potent role in practical life. All these are for the pleasure of God.

ISLAMIC MODEL OF ORGANIZATIONAL EFFECTIVENESS

Based on the above five Islamic qualities the researcher developed Islamic Model for organizational effectiveness. The following chart shows the same:

ORGANIZATIONAL EFFECTIVENESS

PLEASURE OF GOD

PURITY OF HEART

PURITY OF MIND

Islam emphasis on the unity of mankind. The concept of unity arises when the fact that all human beings are from one family, i.e. that Adam, Eve: God also emphasizes on omnipresence and he belongs neither to west and nor to East. He is creator of all human beings. Any kind of bias, prejudices, on the basis of status, caste, community, race, colour, ethnography, etc. and is abhorred.

A manager who internalized all these five qualities for seeking pleasure of God always strikes towards this goal in all aspects of his/her behaviour, be it in life, be it in relationship with his subordinates, colleagues, company policies and work itself. He has acquired meaning of life and work. Work is a way of seeking pleasure of God.

Therefore, the summon bonum of an organization vision and manger's personal life and work life is pleasure of God.

Understanding the Power of Organizational Culture

P.M. AADIL AHMED

The culture of an organization is an amalgamation of the values and beliefs of the people who work there. It can be felt in the unwritten, implicit rules and expectations of behaviour in an organization. It is the unseen force guiding the employees in the expected way. Every organizational culture has values and beliefs that either support or hinder the organizational goals.

If it is positive, the culture of the organization can help to motive staff or at least prevent them from becoming dissatisfied. If the climate does not satisfy the needs of staff, then it will certainly become a demotivator and so people will become less inclined to work towards the organizational goals.

There's been a great deal of literature generated over the past decade about the concept of organizational culture—particularly with regard to changing it. Organizational change efforts are rumored to fail due to lack of understanding about the strong role of culture and the role it plays in an organization.

That's one of the reasons why many strategic planners now place as much emphasis on identifying strategic values as they do for mission and vision.

DEFINITION OF CULTURE

The definition of culture is to impart a flavour of the concept. More formal definitions of culture focus upon the ideologies, norms and customs, shared values and beliefs, which characterized an organization. But a universally accepted definition is almost unthinkable.

Currently, the most widely accepted definition is "a pattern of basic assumptions which invented, discovered or developed by a given group. As it learns to cope with its problems of external adoption and internal integration which has worked well enough to be considered valuable and therefore, to be taught to new members as the correct way to perceive, think and feel in relation to those problems" (Schein; 1985, p. 9). (Retrieved from http://www.bookrags.com/essay-2006/3/28/23628/4446 and accessed on 09.04.2008).

While executive leaders play a large role in defining organizational culture by their actions and leadership, all of the life experiences, strengths, weaknesses, education, upbringing, and so forth of the employees contribute to the definition of organizational culture.

Things in an organization which contribute to the culture or climate:

- The organizational structure of reporting and relationships
- Company policy
- Personnel practices
- Work flow and work loads
- Job design
- Management and supervisory styles

Things which can affect the organizational culture on an individual or personal level :

- Level of trust

- Risk-taking
- Stress
- Fears and anxieties
- Social interaction
- Factions and politics

Some of the principles that can be applied in revitalizing on origination culture are:

- Create jobs to fit people, not people to fit jobs. Apply flexibility, creativity, from and flow in job design
- Encourage autonomy, self-actualization, participation, democratization and shared goals
- Encourage cross-fertilization by specialists seeking wider relevance of their fields of expertise. Encourage choice and change in job roles
- Identity transcends job descriptions
- Cooperation, human values transcend 'winning'
- Blurring of work and play. Work rewarding in itself
- Qualitative as well as quantitative
- Treat employees like adults not adolescents

TYPES OF ORGANIZATIONAL CULTURES

Hofstede *et. al.*; 1990 identified five dimensions of organizational culture in their study:

1. Process-oriented *versus* results-oriented cultures
2. Job-oriented *versus* employee-oriented cultures
3. Open system *versus* closed system cultures
4. Tightly *versus* loosely controlled cultures
5. Pragmatic *versus* normative cultures

1. Process-oriented *vs.* Results-oriented Cultures

Processes-oriented companies have a bureaucratic attitude. All colleagues are looked upon as avoiding taking risk and as spending the least possible efforts. All days are felt to be pretty much the same. On the other hand, the result-oriented ones, employ people who view their colleagues as people who feel comfortable in unfamiliar and risky situations, as people who always do their utmost and who experience each day as a new challenge.

2. Job-oriented vs. Employee-oriented Cultures

In job-oriented organizations, there is a heavy pressure to perform the task even if this is at the expense of the employees. This is because the organization is only interested in the employees produce. In general, decisions are taken by individuals. However, in employee-oriented organizations members of staff feel that their personal problems are taken into account and that the organization takes responsibility for the 'welfare' of its employees, even if this is at the expense of the work.

3. Open System vs. Closed System Cultures

People in a closed system organization will look upon their organization and their colleagues mysteriously. In addition, new employees mostly need more than a year before they feel at home. On the contrary, people in an open system organization have an idea that the organization and the people are very friendly and open to newcomers. Nearly everyone would fit in with the organization, and new employees mostly need few days to feel at home.

4. Tightly vs. Loosely Controlled Cultures

Tight refers to behavioural patterns within the company that are characterized by a strong measure of discipline and supervision. People in companies with tight supervision indicate that everybody is strong cost-conscious that meeting times are kept strictly and that everybody speaks seriously about the company and their job, example's, banks and pharmaceutical companies.

On the other hand, the loose organization is one in which many things are improvised. Loose goes together with less discipline and supervision. People in companies with loose supervision state that nobody thinks of the cost of time and materials, that meeting-times are only kept approximately and that many jokes are made about the company and the job. For example, research laboratories and advertising agencies.

5. Pragmatic *vs.* Normative Cultures

In normative-oriented organization, the emphasis would be on applying the organizational procedures correctly. Besides that, they are generally perceived as having high standards of honesty and business ethics that are upheld, even if this should be done at the expense of the results.

In contrast, in pragmatic organization, the emphasis would be applying on the customer's wishes. They also draw attention to a pragmatic attitude in matters of honesty and business ethics, as the customers themselves will decide what is or is not good for them, they will consider it to their task to serve them as adequately as possible.

PLANT WORLD'S OPERATIONS

Sita, as the founder of Plant World, had combined a life long interest in plants with a botany degree. She had decided what is good and what is not for her company Plant World. Besides that, Sita takes into account customer's wishes, so that the customer could be served satisfactorily.

Every employee in Plant World sees each other as friends. They meet each other twenty minutes before starting to work. In addition, they spent their Sunday with all the colleagues in playing softball, and they assail one another when they were working.

In Plant World, Sita keeps track of the birthdays of all her employees and even those of their children. Besides that, Sita knew that all her employees have family problem, for example, Radha had been up all night with her baby, and Gowry needs to send her sick father. Therefore, she had arranged the schedules so that everyone can work without causing worry to their families. Apart from that, Sita understands her employees when anyone of them simply said, "I don't have a doctor's appointment, I just need the afternoon off". Of all these reasons, all the employees never thought of Sita as the boss or call her any thing but "Sita".

Based on all the characteristic of each dimension, and Plant World's operation, we can describe Plant World as a humanist organization. A humanist organization is the combination of result-oriented culture, employee-oriented culture, open culture, the control towards the employees is loose, and it is pragmatic. The implication is that a humanist organization is likely to be more successful than other organizations that employ non-humanist cultural style of functioning.

PART V

Organizational Development : A Focal View

Organizational Goals and Vision of BHEL—A Case Study

K.S. KRITHIVASAN

"Changes come from small initiatives which work; initiatives which when initiated become the fashion. We cannot wait for great visions from great people, for they are in short supply at the end of history. It is up to us to light our own small fires in the darkness"

—Charles Handy

The activities of a work organization and the management of people are directed towards a variety of goals which are not mutually exclusive and which may conflict with each other. Goals are translated into strategy in order to provide corporate guidelines for the structure and operations of the organization. The power and influence of a business organization must also be tempered by its social responsibilities. Goals, strategy and responsibilities feature in the study of management and organizational behaviour.

An attempt is being made in this paper to present the vision and organizational goals of BHEL as a corporation in general and BHEL, Ranipet in particular as to how the great organization has risen to such a position today.

BHEL

BHEL (Bharat Heavy Electricals Limited) is the largest engineering and manufacturing enterprise of its type in the country and one of the leading power plant equipment manufacturing companies in the world. Having been established in 1963, BHEL offers indigenous design power plant equipment. It has more than 180 products and provides systems and services to meet the needs of core sectors like: power, transmission, industry, transportation, oil & gas, non-conventional energy sources and telecommunication. BHEL has registered a multidimensional growth over the past four decades.

A network spread across the country having 14 manufacturing divisions, 8 service centres, 4 power sector regional centres, 18 regional offices, besides a large number of project sites all over the country and abroad, gives BHEL the advantage of being very close to its customers meeting their specialised needs with total solutions—efficiently and economically. An ISO 9000 certification has given the company international recognition for its commitment towards quality. With an export presence in more than 60 countries, BHEL is truly India's industrial ambassador to the world.

BHEL in Pre-Globalisation Era—Challenges and Threats

In the 1960's and 1970's, BHEL operated in a regulated market environment and the customers (various State Electricity Boards and other utilities) were not allowed to import the power plant equipment. It was practically a monopoly. With the inception of NTPC in 1975 international competition was introduced in line with the stipulations of the World Bank and other multilateral funding agencies. Further in 1991, with the economy opening up and the onset of liberalization/ de-licensing/active encouragement for Foreign Direct

Investment (FDI), the market environment became highly competitive for all products in general

The organizational culture, values and structure were quite strong, the vision and targets (goals) were quite clear. BHEL excellently adapted to the changing environment and set its priorities correctly to face the serious challenges posed to its existence itself. Some of the public sector enterprises could not manage the changing business environment and were getting sick or were even closed. How BHEL managed to float, stabilize, consolidate and rise up is a good case study for any large enterprise to follow. With the demand for electricity always growing, BHEL was committed to the cause of the people in this sector. The motto was "Power to the people". The post-globalization era has seen the tremendous growth of the organization and the challenge today is to sustain and improve.

BHEL in the Last 5 Years

The turnover which was Rs. 8662 crores in 2003-04, has gone up to Rs. 21608 crores in 2007-08. That is an increase of more than 250%. In the same way order book has increased from 16478 crores in 2003-04 to 50268 crores in 2007-08. The profit has gone up from 1017 crores to 4395 crores in the same period. The turnover growth of BHEL, Ranipet is shown below. It has increased by more than 72% in the last two years. This can be attributed only to the leadership, vision and strategies apartment from the commitment of all stakeholders.

FIG. 26.1

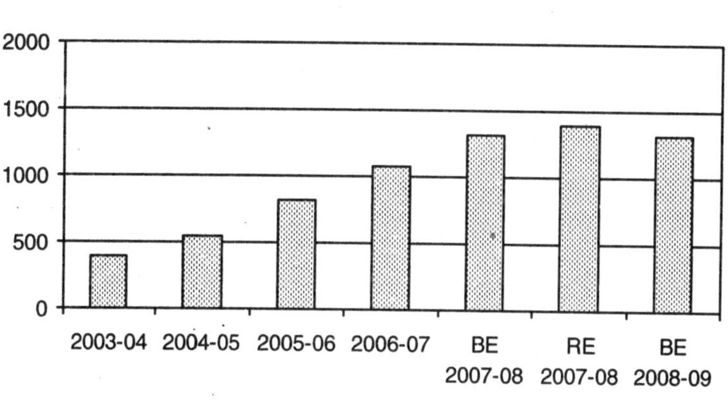

VISION, MISSION AND VALUES

Vision

A World Class Engineering Enterprise committed to Enhancing Stakeholder Value.

Mission

To be an Indian Multinational Engineering Enterprise providing Total Business Solutions through Quality Products, Systems and services in the fields of Energy, Industry, Transportation, Infrastructure and other potential areas.

Values

- Zeal to Excel and Zest for Change
- Integrity and fairness in all matters
- Respect for Dignity and Potential of Individuals
- Strict Adherence to Commitments
- Ensure speed of Response
- Foster Learning, Creativity
- Team-work
- Loyalty and Pride in the Company

FIG. 26.2

Senior leaders have developed and shared the above statements. The vision formulated in 1996 was revised in 2002, then again reviewed in 2006 to reflect the changing business scenario. A typical matrix is shown in Figure 26.2 to explain the process of cascading the vision to individual's performance level.

4. STRATEGIC PLANNING

Strategic planning has been the core strength for the continued business success and growth. The organization has a strategic plan that is current, relevant and prepared with input from all key stakeholders, staff, management, committee, members and community leaders. From time to time the strategies and initiatives have been reviewed and redefined to constantly be in alignment with the Vision and Mission.

- BHEL's strategic plan includes the development of the organization's vision, mission statement, goals and strategies it wants to achieve: When developing the strategic plan, it has been ensured that it is clear and able to be understood by all members of the organization, funding bodies and the broader community.
- Since strategic planning is really about changing attitudes and group action, the goals set are meant to motivate everyone in the organization, to see everyone's efforts are channeled in the same direction with the same broad results in mind.

Setting Organizational Goals

- Goals set describe the broad concerns and strategic direction for BHEL
- They communicate BHEL's intentions to people both inside and outside the organization.
- Goals are challenging but realistic and achievable. They reflect positive change and do not limit flexibility and creativity.
- Even though the goals are for the plan period (3 to 5 years), a procedure has been developed to monitor

them and revise or rework them if the circumstances change.

FIG. 26.3

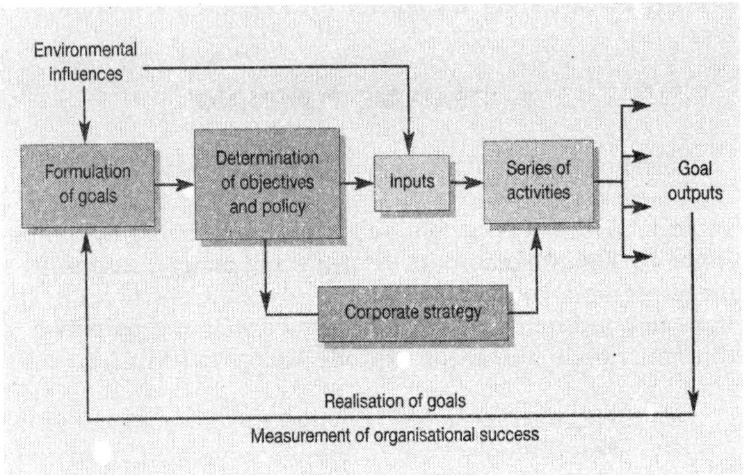

For example some of the targets set for 2008-09 have already been achieved in 2007-08. The strategic plan 2012 for corporate was used to develop the divisional plan 2007-12 for Ranipet Unit. This shows a prospect of more than three-fold turn over increase by 2012. For achieving this, investment plans have been put in place. Detailed risk management processes have also been evolved.

Business Excellence Journey

BHEL/Ranipet have been in the forefront in implementing International system standards like ISO 9001:2000, ISO 14001 and OHSAS 18001. While ISO 9001 is on continual Improvement and enhancing customer satisfaction, the ISO 14001 and OHSAS 18001 has given a thrust in the area of waste minimization, resource conservation, health, safety and environment friendly and sustainable development.

TQM concepts have been used as the vehicle for accelerated journey towards business excellence. From "inspection" in the early 70's, the quality journey today has grown up to encompass Quality Assurance. Reflecting over the past 15 years (since 1993, when first ISO 9001-1987 certification was got), paradigm shifts have been made.

The major changes are:

- From Product Focus . . . to Process focus.
- From over emphasis on documents . . . to creation of suitable processes.
- From inward looking (focus on improvement in manufacturing facility and Technology) . . . to Outward looking (enhanced customer focus—dreaming on behalf of customer).
- Migration from pockets of excellence . . . to Institutionalized synergistic integration and alignment of improvement initiatives.
- From mere conformance . . . to a shift in emphasis towards value addition, asking right questions and challenging *status quo*.
- From viewing non-conformity as a problem . . . to seeing them as opportunities for learning and improvement.
- From quality definition "fitness for use" . . . to customer satisfaction, customer defining quality, win-win situation.
- From role of quality personnel as inspectors . . . to facilitator, change agent, to discover opportunities for improvements as a knowledge provider.
- From individual and departmental success . . . to alignment, stretch, sensitizing key concerns to achieve shared vision.
- From focus on operational effectiveness . . . to focusing on Capability Building.

In our quest for Excellence to achieve product, process and service, cost and quality, leadership started decades ago. Through the journey to Business Excellence, it was learnt to integrate various improvement initiatives, to have sensitive measurement system, to introduce a responsive reward and recognition system, value employees and stakeholders and focus more on the inputs.

The balanced scorecard and e-map align this growth

strategy/key concerns and facilitate assessment and review in an institutionalized manner. The balanced score card combines qualitative and quantitative indicators of performance which recognise the expectations of various stakeholders and relates performance to a choice of strategy as a basis for evaluating organizational effectiveness. Refer Figures 26.3, 26.4 and 26.5 for the charts.

FIG. 26.4
The Balanced Scorecard as a Management System-2

BHEL believes and practices good corporate governance in all its operations and reiterates its commitment to achieve the highest standards. BHEL focuses on enhancement of stakeholder value through adopting proactive measures that brings transparency among the company and its investors, lenders, vendors and customers. Integrity and fairness is one of the values of BHEL. BHEL has joined the Global Compact of United Nations and has committed itself to support it and the set of core values enshrined in its ten principles covering values of human rights, labour standards, environment and anti-corruption.

FIG. 26.5

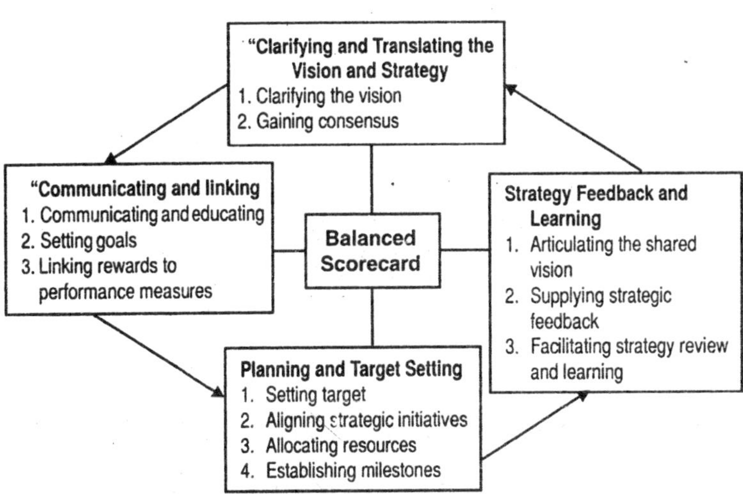

There is compelling shared vision; well laid down strategies; involvement of all employees; excellent technology, processes and facilities; commitment to continuous R&D; Joint working with vendors and sub-contractors; partnership with global companies. The whole process ensures complete coherence and alignment of organizational energy.

Bharat Heavy Electricals Limited is committed to . . . Brightening Lives . . . Powering progress . . . Enhancing Stakeholder Values.

Values, Culture and Strategic Plans of Voorhees College, Vellore

A. ARULAPPAN AND D. PAULRAJ

'Voorhees' is a household name of Vellore and beyond its borders. Many a graduates in the north-western belt of the erstwhile Madras Presidency, now comprising Vellore District, Tiruvannamalai District, Salem District, Dharmapuri District and Erode District mostly were products of Voorhees College, Vellore. It is the alma mater of President of India, Governors, Union Ministers, Union and State Administrators, Literary Scholars, Economists, Social Scientists, Chancellors and Educationists.

Voorhees College, the Premier Educational Institution, was started in 1898 in Vellore. Vellore is the head quarter of one of Tamilnadu's most socially and economically backward district. The College has enviable history and record of being pioneer of Higher Education in the region. The College believes in holistic education in the development of personality of the students. The College is aware of the fact that the students pass through during a short span in their quest to achieve life goals. The College believes in evolving a system for achieving its goals.

In the beginning, the institution was started as an Intermediate College and in a span of eight decades it has grown both as a graduate and post-graduate institution. Research Programmes leading to M.Phil. and Ph.D. degrees have also been started in the post-graduate departments of the College.

The system of education is to provide a sound secular education based on sound Christian values to train young men and women for the service of the country and community. The institution has adhered to this policy to impart the holistic education founded on Christian values and endeavored to inculcate into the hearts and minds of the students. Thus, on sound moral values, the institution stands for building up of the total personality of the individuals on the unchangeable foundation of God.

This paper highlights some of the issues of the Voorhees College which has its roots from western legacy and culture. Voorhees College has been an educational institute imparting strong values to the rural students to become ethically, morally and socially relevant citizens of their country. It is because of a strong institutional culture and ethos espoused by the founder-fathers and the successive leaders and their sustained efforts in building Voorhees College. Over a period of hundred years it has created a culture of synergy which percolated into the life and work of the administrators, staff and students of this college. This has labeled Voorhees College to have had sustainability and adaptability to the changing times and continue to serve the community in the field of higher education.

VALUES AND CULTURE IN VOORHEES COLLEGE

Values and Culture are called Healthy Practices in Voorhees College.

Voorhees College is guided in all its activities by the well-defined statement of purpose and mission.

Mission Statement of the College

"To impart the holistic education founded on Christian values to all students without discrimination especially the less privileged in moulding a character to emerge as self-reliant, enlightened, empowered, change agents of the Society.

"Not some how, but triumphantly" has been the watchword in every word in every step of the College's progress. The College has been subjecting itself to quality and creativity. Planning for development, prioritizing activities and projects to achieve the ultimate vision and keeping pace with the changing trends has been part of life of the College.

GOALS AND OBJECTIVES OF VOORHEES COLLEGE

1. To provide a qualitative holistic education to all students without discrimination for their upliftment in life based on Christian principles.
2. To train these young students in the service of God and Man.

The goals and objectives of the College are stated in the memorandum of Association of Church of South India, Voorhees College, Vellore as well as from time-to-time in the College Calendar.

The institution focuses its attention in promoting the less privileged and marginalized section of the people in the then Madras Presidency particularly in the erstwhile North Arcot district which is considered to be a backward district in the state of Tamilnadu.

All the students are given value-based education with particular reference to caring, sharing and compassion which are the basic Christian principles on which the institution is built.

Value-based Programmes for the Staff and the Students

- Every year at the dawn of the new academic year a staff retreat is conducted. This meeting is arranged at different places every year. A speaker of national and international level specialized in education and leadership skills used to be the speakers. During this kind of meeting members of staff get new insights and renewal of commitment towards their career.
- The college senates regularly exercises itself on quality checks on our academic work by analyzing

examination results, the quality of discipline and the quality of relationships and the events organized in the campus.

- Process for internal quality checks in our College: "Quality checks" are inbuilt at the department level in the area of academic work, conduct of examination and review of results, which promote quality, discipline among students and sound teacher-student relationship.
- Principal conducts extensive discussion with all interested in the welfare of the College and is evolving a master plan for the development of the College. This development if being planned for all areas like academic administration, infra-structural development, starting new courses, growth activities like autonomy and accreditation, exchange programmes and memorandum of understanding with Foreign Universities and value-based education.
- Team work among teachers is cultivated by organizing a number of committees to take care of the multifarious activities of the College. Regular retreat, staff meetings, staff dinners and staff family dinners and staff tours are arranged to foster team work.
- Memorandum of Undertaking is with North Western College, Orange City, Iowa, USA, exchange of academic programmes, summer institutes, internship, faculty exchange are initiated.
- MOU with Sports Development Authority of Tamilnadu, All India Association for Christian Higher Education, New Delhi, and Student Christian Movement—India are initiated and reoriented for the development of the staff and the students.
- At the international level, some of our staff members have attended Advanced Leadership training at Haggai Institute at Singapore and USA. And also presented research papers at international conferences.

Value-based Education

- The College has identified six aspects of a person for the development of his personality. These areas are called PRIMES: an acronym for Physical Resources

Interpersonal, Mental, Emotional and Spiritual development.

- To make our students morally and spiritually sound the college conducts moral and religious instruction classes to inculcate strong moral and spiritual values for life.
- Our College is attempting to impart several social values to enrich the life of the students through various co-curricular and extra curricular activities. In this connection, the role of NSS, NCC, Fine Arts Club, SCM, College Choir, Environmental Club, Student Welfare Council are laudable.
- The College is organizing health awareness programmes and medical checkup campaigns for the benefit of the students.
- Building a great India is one of our thrust areas. To be like "Salt and Light" is always emphasized. Love and pride for the country are continuously incorporated in all our activities. The 'National Anthem', 'Tamil Thai Vazhthu' are part of all the College functions. The Independence Day, the Republic Day and the Flag Day are observed to impart values of democratic India and patriotism.
- Blood donors Club is effectively functioning at our college. Every year at least 150 students donate blood to the Christian Medical College and Government hospital's blood bank.
- Our students participate in the road formation and traffic regulation in Vellore Town.
- NSS activities are always focused on rural development activities.
- Leadership Training is conducted for the Association Secretaries and Student Welfare Council members every year to enhance their skills in communication and organizing.
- The Women's Cell in the college facilitates the women students to have knowledge on the status of women in general, social values, constitutional provisions and rights. The college conducted the following programmes especially for the women students:

  Gender Justice in the new millennium,

Empowerment of Women, and
Seminar on the role of women in the emerging millennium.

VISION OF VOORHEES COLLEGE

The College is planning to pay more attention in the following areas to improve the quality and its efficiency:

- The management is planning to introduce 'Teachers' accountability and Evaluation method' to enhance their performance. This is a self-evaluation mechanism which will help the teachers to identify the areas in their career to improve their performance.
- College will provide internet facilities and electronics library for the benefit of the students.
- College will make efforts to arrange finance support to the poor students to pursue expensive self-finance courses. The College will introduce HRD activities and facilities to improve the personality of the students.
- The College will apply for autonomous status to the college.
- The management of our college has planned to introduce latest courses in the field of Information Technology and Bio-Technology.
- An International Consultation was conducted and it worked out various strategic plans to make the college relevant to the future.

Though Voorhees survived due to strong organizational values and ethos inherited, it has to reorganize its existing infrastructure to augment the facilities so as to become a world class centre with excellence. This is one of the daunting challenges of future leaders of Voorhees. Strong organizational values coupled with sound systems and structure will go together to build an institution to meet the growing demands and requirements of the new era. Therefore, the task is onerous, not only before the management but also from all the stakeholders of Voorhees institution. The corporate spirit and responsibility of all stakeholders in building Voorhees is only panacea for sustainability and adaptability to future challenges.

Organizational Values, Vision and Culture in LIC of India

C.V. Gopal

J.M. Benjamin Jr. in 'Exploiting the values of service over profit in Business (1990)' states: "It is my belief that the purpose of a business is not just to make profit. I believe its fundamental value lies in the social worth of its products and in its impact on the quality of life. It is clear that a business must turn a profit to remain viable, just as a person must eat to live. But people do not live only to eat. A business must also have a large purpose. The total bottom line must measure the total impact of the organization on all the people affected by it".

The exploitation of organizational values must be in two areas. One is the way the organization as a unit interrelates and interacts with the external society, and the other is the value operative in its internal structure and functioning. When the value standards in both these areas are of a high order the organization may be termed an effective value-driven organization. Conceptualizing a good organization is therefore another way of exploiting organizational values. Right attitude to work, principled conduct in work-related activities and pursuit of values by the individual persons forming a team are essential for uplifting the quality of work-life. But in addition to these personal values, the value-climate at the work place is very much shaped by the values pursued and promoted by the organization as a whole. The organization is an entity distinct from the collectivity of its members. Its values are reflected in the goals it sets for itself and in the plans, policies and procedures it follows in its functioning. Organizational values very much depend upon the way the organization looks upon itself. But organizations are not merely formal structures of men, machines and processes created for achieving techno-economic goals. They are also social and human units fulfilling social and human purposes. They affect the quality of life of the persons working in them as well as of the society at large. Hence they must operate within a value framework which is consistent with the larger set of human values and the ethical, social and cultural values of the society. In its relationship with the external world, a dynamic organization sees itself as an agent in the service of the society. This service is performed through fulfilment of an agent in the service of the society. This service is performed through fulfilment of some need or realization of some value that the society considers important for its smooth functioning and growth. For instance, the goal of a Police organization is to enforce law and protect the society from criminals. Educational institutions promote the cause of learning and we at LIC of India meet the various life insurance needs of the Indian society that exists and would arise in the changing socio-economic environment. Apart from covering life risk of Indian citizen, LIC enriches the nation by providing financial assistance to projects associated with power, water supply, transport, housing development, infrastructure development and industrial growth. The citizen's charter of LIC of India speaks clearly about its vision, mission, values, culture, commitment and standards while dealing with customers.

OUR VISION

To transform ourselves into a transnational competitive

financial conglomerate of significance to societies and the pride of India.

OUR MISSION

To ensure and enhance the quality of life of people through financial security by providing products and services of aspired attributes with competitive returns and by rendering resources for economic development.

Our Values	*Our Culture*
Care and courtesy	Agility
Initiatives and Innovative	Adaptability
Integrity	Collaboration
Quality and Returns	Commitment
Participation and Relationship	Discipline
Trust and Reliability	Empowerment
	Sensitivity
	Excellence

OUR COMMITMENT

To the Community: We will:

- Provide insurance cover and financial security to every insurable segment including the social economically weaker sections of the society.
- Meet its insurance needs in consonance with the changing social and economic environment.
- Conduct all aspects of our business keeping in view the interest of the community and the national priorities.

To the Customers: We will:

- Provide them prompt, efficient and courteous service;
- Act as trustees of their funds and invest them to their best advantages;
- Conduct our business with utmost economy and on sound business principles;
- Build and maintain enduring relationships; and

- Keep them informed about our products and services, etc.

To our workforce: We will:

- Promote a sense of participation and make them partners in progress;
- Work towards ensuring job satisfaction and sense of pride;
- Provide an environment and the opportunities for growth to enable them to realize their full potential; and
- Take steps to develop professional skills to enable them to handle their assignments more efficiently.

The Vision and Progress of State Bank of India

P. Anbalagan and M. Lakshmi Priya

SBI is the largest commercial bank in the country with a balance sheet size of over Rs. 315,600 crores supported by a large network of over 9000 domestic branches and 51 branches in 31 countries. The bank has been rate as the best bank in India for the year 2001 by the banker, U.K., and is also the only Indian bank to find a place among the top 20 banks in Asia in terms of tier I capital. This strong capital base supported by technology and skilled manpower allows the bank to take large exposures.

The bank has the largest customer base and offers a wide range of products. With eight banking and seven non-banking associates/subsidiaries in the country, State Bank group is a universal bank and offers a range of services including investment banking, asset management, credit cards, insurance, securities trading and factoring. The bank also has six banking subsidiaries abroad, state bank is a pioneer in many fields—

from financing agriculture and small-scale industry to the recently liberalized insurance sector.

As a premier financial services group with world-class standards and significant global business, the bank is committed to excellence in customer, shareholder and employee satisfaction. "To retain its premier position, the bank will aim at sustained profitability through greater attention to cutting costs, increasing volumes, improving asset quality, expanding fee—based incomes including treasury operations, customized products, and new products, with close attention to risk management and asset liability management".

Objectives

SBI aims to be a one—stop shop for financial products and the bank's foray into fresh fields is in line with its objective to offer a wide range or products to its customers.

Technology

We see technology as the key driver of change. We will fully leverage technology to increase our focus on retail banking and build up volumes through value-added services, achieve efficiency of operations and focus on the needs of all categories of customers with special reference to customers in the younger age group. In due course we propose to integrate on a common site all the arms of the state bank group which would enable cross selling.

Marketing

In the past, the bank's lending was concentrated mainly in industry, which made it vulnerable to any downturn in industry. In the last decade, economic reforms increased income in the economy, particularly in services. At the same time, with increasing competition, customers have also become more demanding. Deregulation offered banks the opportunity to expand the frontiers of their business. All this has increased the scope for consumer finance and retail banking. To leverage its reach covering a large number of consumers all over the country and diversify its asset portfolio, the bank has made consumer finance and retail banking a key focus area. The bank will also focus on infrastructure, enlarging coverage of mid-corporate, trade, housing finance and agriculture.

New Area

The idea is to focus on key areas and support it fully. In the personal banking area, for instance, the bank has set-up a dedicated network of specialized fully computerized personal banking branches, using state-of-the art technology. These branches are targeted personal banking products and services like Internet banking, tele-banking and home banking. The bank will also concentrate on specialized branches for other segments, including commercial branches for mid-corporate, specialized branches for top customers, SSI branches for small industries and hitech agriculture finance branches for high-value agriculture customers.

At the same time, the long-term IT strategy and MIS support will put the bank on a fully integrated technology platform and this will be backed by efficient customer service.

At the outset the majority ownership of SBI has always been with the RBI and SBI has never been owned by the Government. Following financial sectors reforms, this shared has faller in the last ten years from around 98% to 59.7% at present. The remaining 40.3% stake us held by other share-holders including. FIIs, OCBs, NRIs corporates and individuals. However, this has never constrained the bank in its functioning.

With regard to RIB and IMD, SBI has the largest network of international offices among Indian banks, which helps in mobilizing large deposits from investors abroad. All public sector entries are subject to scrutiny by the CVC and SBI is no exception.

Financial Sector Reforms

Since 1990-93, several steps have been taken to strengthen the Indian banking system to make it both viable and efficient. Reserve requirements have been brought down, interest rates deregulated, internationally accepted prudential norms relating to income recognition, asset classification, provisioning and capital adequacy, have been put in place. The share of government in banks' equity has been reduced by allowing nationalized banks to access capital markets, new private banks have come up and the policy towards foreign banks has also been relaxed. In addition, supervision has been strengthened and new institutions such as ombudsman and debt recovery tribunals have been set-up to facilitate debt recovery. The key indicators of banking sector performs during the past few years show that there has been a distinct improvement in the financial health of banks. For example, the net profit of all scheduled commercial banks as a percentage of their total assets has been turned around from a negative figure of minus 1 percentage of an average during 1992-93, 1993-94 to a positive thereafter. Business per employee and profit per employee have also shown improvement and almost all public sector banks have achieved the minimum capital adequacy norm of 9%. The net non-performing assets of scheduled commercial banks as percentage of net advances declined from 7.6% in March 1999 to 6.2% by March 2001.

Now in the second phase of financial sector reforms, the focus is on consolidation, strengthening the legal and institutional framework, risk-based supervision and benchmarking Indian banks more closely with global standards.

Infrastructure Funding Problems

Since infrastructure holds the key to continued economic growth, the Government has taken several policy initiatives over the last few years to facilitate financing of infrastructure in the private sector. There is no statutory ceiling on the amount of term loan that a bank can grant, except of course the normal prudential norm requirements as laid down by RBI, which again have also been liberalized. However, the complexity of the transactions and the large funding requirements, demand an innovative approach towards financial structuring and use of variety of financial instruments. In particular, the relationship between project lender and borrower in such projects make the debt and equity as points in a continuum rather than distinctly separate categories.

In India such financing is usually undertaken by the specialized term lending agencies, particularly IDBI, ICICI, IDFC, IL & FS and IFCI. Commercial banks like SBI rarely take equity positions in projects. It also needs to be clearly understood that lenders are not equity risk-takers and are not in the venture capital business. The lenders are taking a credit risk and they need to be satisfied that they are going to be repaid.

Vision 2020

- To provide bank facilities in rural areas.
- To make bank awareness among citizens.
- SBI has planned to reduce rate of interest.
- To encourage entrepreneur.
- To provide ATM and ALMs to rural branches.

The state banks of India have taken to several steps to strengthen the Indian banking system.

APPENDIX

RAPPORTEURS' SUMMARY

SESSION I
ORGANIZATIONAL VALUES AND BEHAVIOUR

Rapporteur : Dr. S. Bhooma

The first session of the UGC Sponsored National Seminar was chaired by Dr. D. Amarchand, former Professor and Head of Department of Commerce and Registrar, University of Madras, Chennai. He gave an orientation to the participants on the four core value of an organization, viz. Team Work, Honesty, Excellence and Accountability, how they work and how to internalize them.

The first theme session received around 38 papers on the various sub-themes. A paper by Dr. R. Rangarajan and Mrs. A.C. Ranganayaki on Organizational values, vision and culture reiterated the theme of the seminar by stating the importance of values and how one could make them work by having a clear vision, purpose and culture.

Mr. S. Kamaraj spoke of core, stated and protected values in his paper titled 'Organizational values, vision and cultures and its impact on HRD'.

Mrs. C.S. Vijaya stressed the importance of leadership in converting values into performance. This was followed by a presentation by Mrs. G. Tamilselvi on the Organizational Culture present in BPO's—how their non-hierarchical work culture, networked team dynamics and fun culture has brought about a bonding in organisations.

Mr. C.V. Gopal and Mr. Ezilan took up case studies on LIC and ABN Amro (respectively) and analyzed the Value Systems in place in the two organizations, in their respective presentations.

Mr. John Joseph spoke of specific psychometric tests used by LG and Wipro to assess an individual personality so that it creates a 'good fit' with the organization thereby making Indian companies both locally and globally competitive.

Mrs. L. Anusha emphasized that alignment of Organization Values can be brought about by 4P's viz., Purpose, Pride, Persistence and Perspective.

Dr. S. Bhooma made a final presentation on stating how value congruence can be brought about only when the human energies viz. Physical, Intellectual, Emotional and Spiritual, are kindled, and how conflicts can be resolved by tapping the EQ and SQ.

The deliberations raised a pertinent question about the impact of various MNC's on organizational culture and climate and its implication's on society at large. Apprehensions as to whether it would affect the core Indian culture and traditions were allayed by Dr. Mohammed Galib Hussain's fitting reply that India has withstood various cultural invasions in the past and has learned to adapt and adopt from various cultures and has yet managed to retain her distinct Indian cultural identity.

SESSION II
ORGANIZATION GOALS AND VISION

Rapporteur: Dr. R.S. Mani

The second session of the UGC sponsored national seminar was chaired by Mr. K.S. Krithivasan, Additional General Manager, BHEL, Ranipet. He has highlighted the problems, competition, need importance and growth of BHEL Ranipet on the prospective of organizational values, vision and culture. He described about RADAR approach and SMART approach. He also discussed the Balance scorecard, E. MAP system connected with the corporate strategy. He explained about 'IMPRESS' system connected with productivity followed in BHEL. He stated about synergy integration, zeal to excel and faster learning organization.

There are 18 participants presented their papers on various dimensions connected with the topic. Ms. Natesan Bhooma read about the core values, strong and weak culture existing in the organisations. Dr. M. Samsudeen explained about the relationship between the productivity and Islamiah culture. He stated about five factors such as sincerity, patience, forgiveness, mutual consultation, love and affection of Islamic culture, with productivity.

Prof. Mr. S. Abdul Sajid of Melvisharam stressed the importance of specific values and management styles connected with organization culture and detailed its impact on organizational culture.

Mr. T. Retivakumar spoke on organizational culture values, vision and mission. He narrated various ways to overcome the problems that the organization will come across while evolving goals and visions.

Mr. K. Balaji stressed the importance of the organizational culture, vision, goals and values, while monitoring the adherence of values.

The discussions highlighted the following problems such as corporate challenges, wrong accountability, ego, stress and absence of organizational culture among management and employees. It has also thrown a light on inadequate infrastructure.

The participants has also explained about how to overcome the aforesaid problems through participating in work culture conducting culture interviews, insisting on safety measures, empowering employees to take decisions on their own. They elaborated the best reviewing approach for improving the organizational goals.

Dr. Anbalagan introduced the Chairperson and Mr. Ezhilan welcomed the gatherings.

SESSION III
OVVC IN INSTITUTION OF HIGHER LEARNING

Rapporteur : A. Dhanalakshmi

The third session of the UGC sponsored National Seminar was chaired by Dr. H.R. Venkatesha, Director, Archarya Institute of Science—Centre for Management Studies, Bangalore. He has highlighted that the global scenario of the quality of education and questioned whether our educational system is able to cope with the global standards. He had clearly mentioned the *status quo* of the higher education. He emphasized that the educational institutions should equip the students to face the forthcoming knowledge economy. He also insisted that the educational institutions should try to fill the gaps among the educational institutions, students and technology. He expressed that there is misconception that quality is very costly in fact, it is very cheap. The quality of education should be student centric. He had suggested that a system should evolve a mechanism to specialize faculty members in few subjects/areas so that they become experts in that area so that they can deliver quality education and impart values among the students and prepare them face the global competition.

He expressed that the regulatory bodies should not interfere in deciding the syllabus for students rather it should be decide by both the students and teachers based on their need of the hour. In short, it should be students' centric. Finally, he stressed that we have to welcome the foreign universities, and also invest in FDI. Also attract the efficient academicians throughout the globe for the enrichment of our future students.

The third theme session received around 15 papers on various sub-themes.

Prof. Francis in his paper on "Value of Human Relationship in the educational institutions" emphasized that there should be a proper balance between sharing and shouldering the authority and responsibility respectively among the educationalists. The role played by the people in the organization is indispensable for the development of the organizational culture and vision. He concluded by stating that participative style of leadership will help educational institutions to provide quality education in present global scenario.

Dr. Mohideen, highlighted 15 cultural values and beliefs based on the Islamic culture.

Dr. Arulappan, examine the values, vision and culture in Voorhees College, emphasizing team work and moral instruction.

Mrs. Padmaja, stressed the role of manager is creating conscious organizational culture and emphasized on stress coping strategy adopted by the managers.

Dr. P. Ebenezer Benjamin highlighted social security aspect of the Home-based workers of the Beedi industries in Vellore district, Tamil Nadu, who comprise 90.33% of total beedi work force and 9.33 times of workers employed in the industrial premises.

Mr. T. Afsar Basha highlighted effectiveness and ineffectiveness of an organization based on their cultural patterns developed on the basis of humanistic psychoanalysis.

Mr. A. Nelson Vimalanathan stated that Voorhees College has cherished its goals and practiced the values with future growth and development. The visionaries (founding fathers) with a missionary zeal created the institution and Voorhees College survived for more than 100 years because of its strong cultural values and ethos.

The deliberations raised a pertinent question about the impact of various MNC's on organizational culture and climate and its implications on society at large. Apprehensions as to whether it would affect the core Indian culture and traditions were allayed by Dr. H.R. Venkatesha, fitting reply that India has withstood various cultural invasions in the past and has learned to adapt and adopt from various cultures and has yet managed to retain her distinct Indian cultural identity.

SESSION IV
BUILDING A WORLD CLASS ORGANISATION

Rapporteur : Dr. M. Akbar Mohideen

I express my great sense of gratitude to the Lord, All Benevolent and all merciful and I express my thanks to our most respected Prof. M. Anbalagan, the HOD of Commerce & the Organizing Secretary of this National Seminar for given me an opportunity to perform the pleasant duty of Rapporteur for the Theme Session IV.

The IV Session was strated by 2.00 p.m. on 16th April, 2008. The Chair Person of this session Prof. Dr. Mohammed Ghalib Hussain, HOD of Corporate Secretaryship, Islamiah College,

Vaniyambadi, with his versatile knowledge and experience delivered a thought provoking speech about the theme. He has enlightened the theme in various angles and articulated "how to build" aspect of world class Indian business organisations. He was beautifully quitted the examples of successful Indian Organisations such as Bajaj Auto, Hindustan Liver Ltd., Telco, Mahindra and Mahindra Ltd., Reliance Group and Godrej Group. He has touched the theoretical and philosophical underpinning of vision formation of the above companies in the light of Hindu mythology. He further narrated the Indian contributions such as Management by Values by S.K. Chakraborthy, Management by Trust by R.S. Dwivedi and his own alternative approach to management termed Management By Faith and its theoretical framework for building world class organisation. His electrifying speech made the audience spell bound and impressed every one present in the seminar.

Followed by the Chairman's speech the following papers were presented:

1. Mr. S. Sathianathan Prasanna, HOD, Dept. of Business Administration, Voorhees College, Vellore, presented a paper on "Emerging New Trends in Modern Organisations with reference to BPOs. He stressed that, money has assumed the position of God in BPOs. He very beautifully brought out the family values of Indian Society are being eroded in BPOs.
2. Mr. E. Meiyappan, Lecturer, SG in Commerce and Mr. M. Gnanamurugan, Lecturer in Commerce, Arignar Anna Govt. Arts College, Cheyyar presented a paper on "The Impact of Motivation and Morale in organizational Culture". They brought out the relationship of Motivation and Morale to the Organizational Culture. They conclude that the Motivation and Morale increases the effectiveness of organizational culture.
3. Mr. V. Gunasekaran & Ms. S. Sakthi Saral, Lecturers, Dept. of Business Admn. and Dr. D. Kothandaraman, Reader, Dept. of History, Voorhees College, Vellore presented a paper on the topic "Organizational Culture and Leadership". They conclude, culture is created by

the absence of the leader and is also embedded and strengthened by leader.

4. Ms. V. Senbaga Priya, HOD of Commerce, Marudhar Kesari Jain College for women, Vaniyambadi, presented a paper on "Employee Retention Strategy". She focused on the retention strategy by giving training, proper incentives and motivational measures. These measures bind the employees to stick on the same organisation.
5. Dr. J. Srinivasan, Lecturer (SS) in Commerce, Arignar Anna Govt. Arts College, Cheyyar presented a paper on "Enhancing Corporate Culture through 360-Degree Feedback". He has brought out 360-degree conceptualization, 360-process implementation of 360-degree feedback to enhance corporate culture and the method of implanting 360-degree feedback in companies.
6. Mr. S. Balamurugan, HOD of Commerce, Mano College, Cheranmahadevi, Tirunelveli, presented a paper on "The Impact of Culture on International Organizational Behaviour". He has highlighted that, culture differences must be recognized in understanding organizational Behaviour.
7. Mr. S. Kamalakannan, Guest Lecturer, Dept. of Commerce, Govt. Arts College, Tiruvannamalai, presented a paper on "Building Organizational Culture that Stimulates Creativity". He has emphasized the role of values, behavioural characteristics and modes for the professionals.
8. Mr. R. Ganesan, HOD of Commerce, M.G. Arts College, Vellore, presented a paper on "Organizational Culture—A Critical Review". He has pointed out there are three types of Cultures viz. National Culture; Organizational Culture and Business Culture and beautifully highlighted the development of culture in an organization.
9. Ms. R. Subashini, Lecturer; Ms. N. Dhivspriya and Ms. M. Venkata Chaitanya, Student, VIT Business School, VIT University, Vellore presented a paper on "Ideal Corporate Culture for a Perfect Tomorrow".

They have highlighted the significance of corporate culture and threw light on the leadership.

10. Dr. S. Kayalvizhi, Assistant Professor, School of Management, C. Abdul Hakeem College of Engineering & Technology, Melvisharam, presented a paper on "VISTAT—Vision of TATA group". She has rightly touched the theme of the session by highlighting the vision of the TATA group with a case study. The paper has brought out the core values of the TATA group.
11. Ms. Lakshmi Jagannathan, Asst. Professor and Ms. P.R. Akila, Lecturer, Dept. of Management Studies, Dayanandha Sagar College of Engg., Bangalore submitted a paper on "The Impact of Globalization on ethics in Indian Business". The paper dealt with the impact of western forms on the ethics and values on Indian organization. The paper further suggests strategies to combat these influences.
12. Ms. K.G. Hemalatha Asst. Professor and A. Dhanalakshmi, Senior Lecturer, Dept. of Management Studies, Dayanandha Sagar College of Engg., Bangalore presented a paper on "The role of culture in Multinational Context". They emphasize the influence of the Multinational Companies on Indian business. They opine managers have to understand the relationship between the National Culture and Organizational Culture. To bring out the above point a case study of Hungarian Multinational Organization is presented.
13. Ms. R. Hemavathy, Staff, VIT University, Vellore presented a paper on "A Study on Organizational climate with reference to BHEL, Ranipet". She has highlighted the organizational culture and climate prevailing in the organization. She has pointed out the worker's attitude towards job satisfaction, job security, salary, welfare measures safety, etc.
14. Ms. L. Sofia, HOD of Commerce, Immaculate College for Women, Viriyur, presented a paper on "Organizational Values Vision & Culture". She has pointed out the importance of values, vision and

culture in any organization. She has concluded that the culture has such an impact that it can make or break any organization's success.

Many of the papers that have been presented are nothing but treasure boxes over-loaded with electrifying thoughts. I am of the firm belief that the sparks of brilliant ideas and blazing opinions that have been raised here will illumine the prospects of values, vision and culture and will surely reshape the destiny of the organisations involve in these activities.

Index